NOVICE WITCHES AND APPRENTICE WIZARDS

An essential handbook of magic

First published in 2022 by Liminal 11

© 2021 White Star s.r.l.
Piazzale Luigi Cadorna, 6
20123 Milano, Italia
www.whitestar.it

Written by Francesca Matteoni

Illustrated by Elisa Macellari

Project and Editorial Coordination
Balthazar Pagani

Editing
Caterina Grimaldi

Graphic Design
Sebastiano Girardi Studio

Editorial Assistant and Page Layout
PEPE *nymi*

Translation: Iceigeo, Milan (coordination: Lorenzo Sagripanti;
translation: Alexa Ahern)
Editing: Phillip Gaskill

Liminal 11 Edition:
Art Director: Kay Medaglia
Cover Design: Fez Inkwright
Designer: Tori Jones

Printed in China

ISBN 978-1-912634-55-2

10 9 8 7 6 5 4 3 2 1

www.liminal11.com

FRANCESCA MATTEONI

NOVICE WITCHES AND APPRENTICE WIZARDS

An essential handbook of magic

ILLUSTRATIONS BY ELISA MACELLARI

INTRODUCTION
THE VEIL OF APPEARANCES
p. 6

HISTORY OF MAGIC
p. 9

WITCHES AND WIZARDS
p. 31

INSTRUMENTS
p. 81

ANIMALS
p. 113

PRACTICES AND SPELLS
p. 145

BIBLIOGRAPHY AND BIOGRAPHY
p. 158

THE VEIL OF APPEARANCES

✷ ✷ ✷

How many times in life have we wished for our greatest desires to come true *like magic*, to erase unpleasant situations *like magic*, to travel wherever we want *like magic*? And without much effort or serious commitment. What is magic, exactly? Who knows how to use it, practice it?

The history of different populations around the world tells us that magic has always existed. At first glance, almost everything is magic: the lightning that sets a tree on fire; the blowing, singing, raging wind; the bubbling, reflecting, flowing stream; the seed breaking through the soil to blossom. The invisible entities that animate fire, air, water, and earth are magical. The words and gestures we use for them are magical.

Magic is not an easy gift at all. It is complex because it requires one to lift the veil of appearances and touch the soul that resides in everything. It has always been a tool for understanding the secret ties between things and learning the language of these connections. Those who can speak the language have been considered many things: powerful and respectable, evil and dangerous, deceptive and cunning, poetic and wise, dreamers and warriors. Those who think of the world as magical today are able to listen. They don't reject feelings of any kind. They prefer the difficult route over the easy one. They accept the existence of pain, struggle, fear alongside celebration, joy, and hope. Magic is not detached from reality; it is immersed in it. It draws a trail in both the exterior and interior reality, which might seem separate but are in fact connected. One is the mirror image of the other.

This book was created for anyone who wishes to follow the trail of magic to learn about its history, important figures, objects, and of course some of the fundamental principles of the magical arts through its practices and rituals. It was created because the authors believe there is a need for magical acts, which can re-establish ties and lost affection between humans and all the plant, animal, and mineral beings that inhabit our Earth, which should be protected as if it were a gift. *The* gift.

The first part of the book delves into the magical history of the Western world, from ancient times to the rebirth of witchcraft in modern times. We will meet with fortune-tellers, wizards, witches, and alchemists. We will encounter spirits, potions, and prophecies, as well as burnings at the stake and hangings—for decades, magic was seen as a horrendous beast that needed to be wiped out, condemning and killing thousands of people, innocent victims of the political, religious, and social system of the era.

In the second part, we will get to know witches and wizards in the flesh, some who were real people and others who lived in mythology and literature. They will tell us our future, heal us, show us the music of the planets, try to make us drink love potions, speak to us about invisible masters, goddesses, and plant spirits.

In the third part, we will discover certain animals: those that served as companions to witches and wizards, and those that are special creatures with their own magical and even prophetic characteristics. We must always treat them with respect and kindness, which doesn't mean we should tame all of them. Magic teaches us that sometimes even distance is an act of love.

In the fourth part, you will be given some tools for performing magic. As many contemporary authors write, all you need is the sky above, a field below, or the seashore. All you need is to collect a few shells, find a rock with a hole, or create a candle. Lastly, in part five, you can read and test some spells that aim to help you make peace with your past and your destiny by trying to contemplate and embrace before revolutionizing and dismissing.

Magic reaches the stars, it's true, but it's slow-moving like a tree, which looks almost immobile as its roots and branches breach the worlds above and below. In the book, images accompany your reading, tickling the imagination.

Read the book from beginning to end, or dive in wherever you like. There are no specific rules. Explore it on the surface, or more deeply. I hope the most genuine magic you gain is stepping more lightly on our Earth, because she is our beating heart.

HISTORY OF
MAGIC

Magic inhabits the threshold
of society. Those who frequent
this threshold are either
marginalized or respected.
They embody fears, desires, and
mysteries. In this chapter, we
will trace the history of magical
arts from the beginning to the
medieval era, through the early
modern period of great wizard-
philosophers and witches burned
at the stake, and up to more
recent centuries when magic has
become a personal practice of
healing and awareness.

SEERS, ORACLES, AND WITCH DOCTORS
OF THE ANCIENT WORLD

∧ ∨ ∧ ∨ ∧

Magic is traditionally used to understand and manipulate nature, and to contact spirits and the invisible. In the culture of the Ancient Egyptians, we find the concept of *heka*, a force that animates and holds up the cosmos. It was used by both divine beings and common people, to whom it was passed at a time when the boundaries between the divine and human were weak, and a dialogue between the two was constant. In the Mesopotamian region, the first traces of witches emerged. These individuals performed spells with the help of demons who were hostile toward humans and always ready to attack them. In general, knowing the names of demons in magical practices meant you could control them, and amulets and rituals were used to fend off witches' spells. In Greece, we first encounter the word "magic." It was here that those who performed magic were priests of the Zoroastrian religion from nearby Persia. These figures were administrators of the sacred and readers of dreams. It was three Magi (the name for Zoroastrian priests) who brought gifts to the Christian baby Jesus after following a comet through the desert. These priests and priestesses were interpreters of signs and miracles, all-knowing figures who could anticipate future events. This was the case of well-known female oracles, like the Pythia, who interpreted prophecies over the vapors of a hidden spring under the Temple of Apollo at Delphi. There was also the Cumaean Sibyl, who wrote prophecies on leaves in a cave near Naples. (Every prediction was obscure, since she was translating from the language of the gods, which contained a poetic and symbolic alphabet.)

Poetry is another form of magic, as is seen with the poet Orpheus, who could heal with the sound of his harp and voice.

His failed attempt to bring his wife Eurydice back from the Underworld is the origin myth of the Orphic Mysteries, whose initiates were promised a ritual cleansing that would allow them to return to life after death.

These figures were sometimes considered priests of the divine, but sometimes also possessed aspects that were unpopular with religions and official sects because they were necromancers, soothsayers, herbalists, or could speak to the dead and understand the secrets of nature. In the *Book of Leviticus* from the Torah and Old Testament, alongside visions of the prophets, we find the following quote, prohibiting believers from seeing such magical figures: "Do not turn to mediums or necromancers; do not seek them out, and so make yourselves unclean by them: I am the Lord your God." From God, miracles are derived; from witches, only tricks. In Rome in 13 BCE, the emperor Augustus had two thousand magical manuscripts burned. The Roman philosophers defined magic as the most fraudulent of arts, and those who practiced magic were subversive figures who harnessed the occult powers of nature.

And yet, people continued to seek out magic to fight the evil eye, to bewitch their beloved, to protect themselves from illness, and even to curse others. Statuettes, boards, and amulets are concrete proof. In the Mediterranean region, magical practices persisted throughout antiquity, starting in the 5th century BCE with the tradition of the witches of Thessaly: experts in potions whose arts were considered so powerful that they could draw down the moon from the sky as they pleased. One of them was the literary figure Erichto, a necromancer who lived in a tomb. She was invented by the Roman poet Lucan and reappeared in Canto IX of Dante's *Inferno*. These witches seemed to possess something special and represented the great confusion that existed between the divine, magic, the natural, and the supernatural in the culture of that time.

Predatory and mysterious, witches were often associated with owls. Winged demons and female demons merged in Middle Eastern beliefs. For example, there was Lilith from Mesopotamia, whereas in Greece Lamia was a serpentine specter of a woman who died prematurely and who harassed children and young men. The Roman *strix*, nocturnal birds that drank blood and ate the bodies of infants, derived from these figures.

Masca is another name for demon witches, and was used along with "strix" up until the Middle Ages. They flew about, visited homes at night, drank blood, and kidnapped children. Among Germanic populations, these figures were increasingly humanized, thriving on the prophetic legends connected to the deities known *amatronae*. The historian Tacitus said that the Germanic peoples believed something sacred resided in women, and therefore, female advice was held in high regard. The difference, however, between sacred and demonic resided in the flap of a wing in the night or a cry that transformed a vision into a nightmare.

BURNINGS AND DEMONS: THE GREAT WITCH HUNT

∧ ∨ ∧ ∨ ∧

When we think of witches, we imagine an old woman and her animal companion brewing concoctions, wandering through cemeteries, and flying on broomsticks. Another image that comes to mind is that of those hanged and burned at the stake centuries ago.

The female stereotype of the witch as an evil-doer who causes harm—in opposition to a good mother who is tender and caring—is inextricably tied to the great witch hunt that occurred in Europe and the American colonies between the 15th and 18th centuries. It sentenced to death tens of thousands of people. Although most were women, it wasn't exclusively so. Whoever practiced witchcraft could be condemned, and in some

places, like Normandy and Estonia, the number of persecuted men was higher than that of women.

As we've seen, witchcraft is an ancient belief, and witches were in every corner of the globe. What they had in common were the following characteristics:

* They used supernatural methods to harm members of their community.
* They were marginalized and acted in secret, driven by their innate wickedness.
* They followed a specific tradition which was inherited through a certain type of apprenticeship.
* They could be fought with acts of counter-magic that revealed their identity and forced them to use their power to heal, destroying them physically.

At a certain point in Western history, first in Europe and then in the American colonies of New England, witches officially became public enemies of institutions. They had to be persecuted and exterminated by any lawful means. This occurred when all the characteristics mentioned above were connected to a religious element. From that point on, witches were seen as individuals who not only cast spells but were also allies and servants of Satan himself, assisting him in his fight to destroy Christian society.

At this point, biblical admonitions against witchcraft were recovered and used to justify social persecution. The most famous verse used for this comes from Exodus: "Thou shalt not suffer a witch to live."

Following these words and urged by the German inquisitor Heinrich Kramer, Pope Innocent VIII issued a terrible document, the papal bull *Summis Desiderantes Affectibus*, which was used to establish the heretical nature of witches and give orders to suppress them. A few years later, Kramer published *Malleus Maleficarum*, a text steeped in misogyny that states that women are more inclined to wicked influences because they are weak, inferior, and sinful. The witch hunt only got worse, growing due to religious conflicts that exploded soon after in Europe between Catholics and Protestants. It was crueler in some countries, including Switzerland, France, and Germany.

According to theories of demonology from that time, witches caused plagues, shipwrecks, and natural disasters. They would gather at night sabbaths in remote, enchanted places, like the walnut tree of Benevento, Italy, or the mysterious Blåkulla Island in Sweden, which could be reached only by flying. During these gatherings, they had sexual relations with demons, ate human flesh, and prepared salves and potions. They then made a pact with the Devil, selling their souls. This pact left an unspecified mark on the body—any sort of anomaly, from a freckle to a scar, which was believed to not sense pain and didn't bleed when pricked. This was used as a perverse way to reveal that someone was a witch, along with methods of torture that coerced confessions out of them.

In English records, this mark was left by a familiar, a demon spirit in animal form, that the witch fed with their own blood and other things (milk, bread, beer, etc.). One common theory was that witches could transform into animals like hares, ravens, and cats. Then they would freely roam about, committing evil deeds like knotting the hair of horses, stealing milk, and sucking the breath from infants. After all, the Devil had hooves and goat horns, closely resembling the Greek god Pan. Witchcraft merged with figures from the Pagan world, which were distorted into something evil that continuously threatened and harassed the human soul that had been washed and purified by the sacrificial blood of Christ, according to official religious creed.

In reality, accusations didn't take into consideration serious social issues or grave disasters. Instead, witches were blamed for illnesses that afflicted cattle and infants.

If a cow wouldn't give milk, it was because of a curse; if a child was sick, it was because someone had jinxed them. Some traditional, magical stories were exceptions to the most common accusations, like that of the tempestarii—witches and wizards of the sea who could release storms. In Finland, wizards sold winds to sailors in the form of knots, loosening and tying them to control their strength. On the islands off Sicily and in the seas beyond, there were formulas that allowed one to break the whirlwinds on the waters.

One thing, however, is definitely real: for more than two centuries, many innocent people were condemned to death. The fear-mongering of this climate even led presumed witches to visit hangmen to have themselves examined for marks of the Devil. But even in such unfortunate times, were all witches considered instruments of Satan?

HEALERS, FAIRIES, AND NIGHTLY GATHERINGS

∧ ∨ ∧ ∨ ∧

"Those who heal can also destroy" and vice versa, stated a Latin maxim. Even though the issue of witchcraft raged everywhere, seeping into all cultures—and proof of this part of history unfortunately comes from records of trials—not all witches were feared and driven away.

The line between magic and healing is subtle, and wise women and men—let's call them "benevolent" witches and wizards—were even consulted for various reasons, like to create herbal remedies; find lost or stolen goods; create love potions,

divinations, and amulets; perform acts of counter-magic against curses; and disarm evil witches. Rufina dello Sbardellato, from Pitigliano in Tuscany, was called "Saint Rufina" by the people of her village because she knew how to work the healing properties of herbs, although she was later accused of witchcraft. In England, those who practiced the magic profession for beneficial purposes were called "cunning folk", and were mainly men. They had a repertoire of formulas and written charms, which often included the names of Jesus, the Virgin Mary, and Saint Peter. Some, like John Walsh, claimed they had learned magic from some powerful book... which we could guess was the Bible itself, since the sacred and magical were one and the same in the collective imagination. They were asked anything, from important life questions to simple foolishness, for magical cures for sick loved ones to solutions for shabby clothes (since back then, wardrobes certainly weren't overflowing with garments).

The cures of witches followed the medical knowledge of that time, when laxative tablets and herbal teas were prescribed in the belief that bodies were liquid and the proper functioning of the blood and bodily fluids determined not only physical but also spiritual health. Some elements of magical cures would seem strange and unbelievable to the modern reader. For example, love potions common in Catholic areas contained animal and human parts, like menstrual blood, donkey brain, sperm, hair, and, in some Spanish formulas, the bones of cats and humans. In England, to free oneself of a curse, there was the "witch bottle," which was filled with urine, hair, and fingernails from the victim of the presumed curse, along with pins, needles, splinters of iron or wood, and thorns. The bottle was sealed and heated over fire, or buried. At that point, the witch would have either shown up at the door of the victim or fallen ill on the spot. What explanation did they give for this practice? Well, the bits of body parts and liquids from the victim of a spell placed in the bottle were also vital substances of the witch. In the spell, the souls and bodies of the witch and victim were united. The victim inverted the process in the bottle by taking back control—burning, piercing, suffocating, and causing intolerable pain to the witch.

Some denominations, however, tell a different story from that of the pact with the Devil. They suggest that a world independent of beliefs and traditions existed and persisted beneath the ashes of the burnings carried out by Christianity. In Scotland and in Sicily under Spanish rule, witches were believed to receive advice and powers from fairies who lived on hills and in open spaces. The Sicilian *Donas de fuera* were fairy-like beings who would meet "in spirit" at nightly gatherings. In Scotland, fairies could appear before witches, sometimes marking them with a scar on the forehead or signs of biting and scratching. The nature of fairies was ambiguous, mixed with the spirits of the dead; with the remains of primitive and ancestral tribes scattered throughout the landscape; with the Christian theories of fallen angels. In Ireland, there were no witch trials because fairies—non-human, and therefore non-prosecutable, beings—were responsible for altering the fates of individuals and their possessions.

One of the more complex traditions that expands the idea of benevolent witchcraft is that of the benandanti in the Friuli region of Italy from the 16th and 17th centuries. These "good walkers" were men and women who knew the art of magical healing, and would leave their bodies at night to fight evil witches and wizards in the fields to protect the health of the living and secure the season's harvest. When they were tried in the Inquisition, they defended themselves by claiming their devotion to God, in whose name they acted, having been visited and encouraged to fight by angels, his messengers. In their fascinating stories, the agrarian cults and Catholic magic blended, along with the power of the soul to travel through dreams, leaving behind the body. Were these only fantasies, or the result of conditioning? This tangle of stories is difficult to unravel, but one narrative thread emerges: the existence of a physical cosmos that was held together by the spiritual, religious, magical, and arcane. Here, you are as likely to save yourself as you are to lose yourself.

THE SOUL OF THE WORLD AND THE SECRETS OF WIZARDS

∧ ∨ ∧ ∨ ∧

Cults, rituals, and popular fears found their perfect opposite in the cultured thinking of the Renaissance. A higher magic existed alongside the witches and healers, one that spoke directly to the order of creation. Wizards brushed shoulders with philosophers, physicians, and even priests and theologians.

This melting pot of traditions and influences shaped the erudite mentality of that time, which brought about the notion of the existence of an energy understood to be the love that permeates creation. At the beginning of the 14th century, the greatest poet of that era (and many other eras), Dante Alighieri, recognized that love transcends our mortal nature, leading us toward the divine. According to the *Divine Comedy*, God is "the love that moves the sun and other stars." This beautiful image says a lot about the philosophical science that the poet was immersed in. There is a spirit that binds all beings, animating them, moving the stars and planets, descending into the flesh, and lifting you to view the sacred. This echoes the concepts of Christian compassion and the Kabbalah tree of life, which claim that a life force radiates from the heavenly

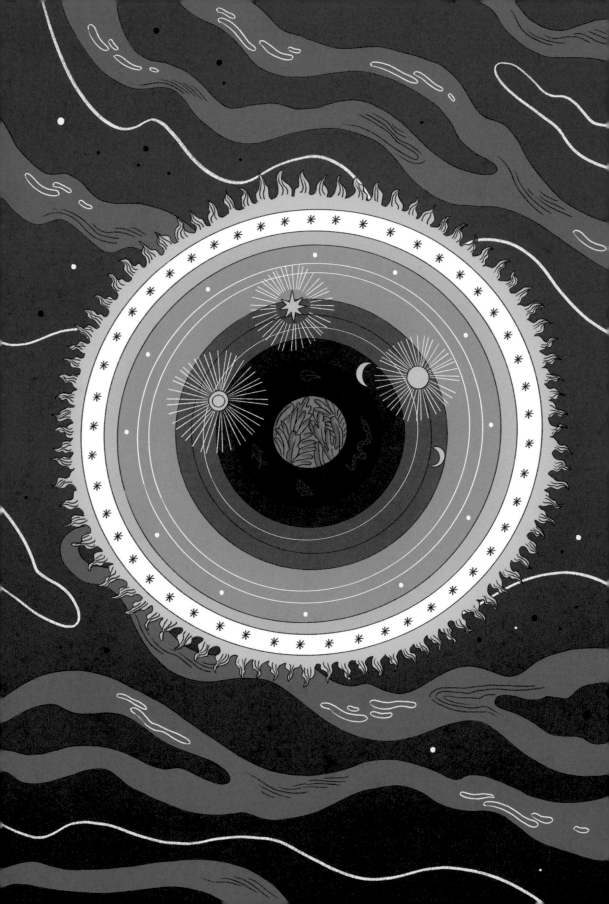

spheres down to earth—but the same is true in the opposite direction. This was the case of Plotinus's Neoplatonism, described in his *Enneads*, in which praying to divine beings and magic worked together to unite the universe. This was the soul of the world. From a purely humanistic approach, we can say that the universe is like a large body in which physical and intellectual substances, as well as those of the soul, work together, but we can also say that the work of the universe can be deciphered in the human body. This interpretation is found in astrology, which states that celestial bodies directly influence Earthly life and the physical and behavioral temperaments of its inhabitants. As a science, astrology derives from Greek philosophy, and more specifically from Aristotle. The divine plan was realized on Earth thanks to the influence of the stars and planets, which were made up of a fifth element, "ether", a spiritual and life-giving substance.

Natural magic, which was defended by Renaissance-era intellectuals like Marsilio Ficino and Pico della Mirandola, was a cognitive tool used to investigate the invisible bonds between the microcosm and macrocosm. The soul united the body and mind in humans, and likewise the soul of the world united physical matter and the divine principle. Natural magic, which was introspective, saw value in the spirit of things beyond their transitory nature. Natural magic, therefore, brought together astrology and medicine since it could be used to cure humanity. And the wizard was its keeper.

With burnings at the stake a distant memory, magic as a sacred science was able to illuminate the Earthly path. And the greatest sacred science was alchemy. Alchemists were known for being experts in metals and medicine. They worked (and work) in secret on the Great Work, the search for the philosopher's stone, which could transmute metal into pure gold. Alchemy was widespread, from China and India to the Mediterranean Basin, and was based on humans' search for immortality—the subject of one of the oldest stories in the world, which has been passed down in pieces: the Sumerian-Babylonian epic of Gilgamesh, a hero who went on a journey in search of the plant of immortality at the bottom of the sea.

Immortality, like gold, carries a deep, mystical meaning for alchemists and requires self-sacrifice, study, and faith. In the 13th century, the friar and alchemist Roger Bacon wrote that "alchemy is a science that teaches you to transform any type of metal into another," proving himself to be a forefather of modern chemistry. The key to this transformation was the idea that the same spirit or energy could be accessed in all substances. This elixir was as important to alchemy as the philosopher's stone. The elixir of life—"nectar" to Greco-Romans or *amrit* to Hindus—later blended with the legend of the Holy Grail from Medieval Christian mythology. The mysterious cup gave whomever drank from it eternal youth. Jesus drank from the Grail at the Last Supper, and Joseph of Arimathea was said to have collected his blood in it.

Alchemy interpreted existence as the transformative process of the digestion of matter, rotting, and rebirth. Understanding immortality meant seeing the naked truth, reuniting the individual soul with the universal soul. It was represented by the "Cauda Pavonis," a phenomenon that created a temporary sparkle of all colors in an alchemical still. It predates the distillation of the elixir and the attainment of the philosopher's stone. For alchemists, God was everywhere, the spiritual seed planted in the dark earth, a trace of the soul in matter.

However, not even this form of magic was free of suspicion and accusations of fraud, and of course, not all wizards were honest. Some used their knowledge simply to make ends meet... not unlike today.

DRAWING DOWN THE MOON:
WITCHES AND WIZARDS TODAY

∧ ∨ ∧ ∨ ∧

The arts of high magic and as well as witchcraft both allowed one to peer through darkness, the former with wisdom and the latter with intuition. One was affected by hope, whereas the other, at least on a social level, was affected by fear. One was cultured and intellectual; the other was wild and unpredictable. What might have been the result of their collaboration?

The answer began to appear in the 19th century when interest in the occult—which was never fully repressed—began to thrive again. Initiatory societies had survived long after the witch hunts, just like divination and healers, whose profession never disappeared despite banishment. In London in the 18th century, Freemasonry was officially founded. It was the most secret society and was based on the fraternal ties among members, who strived to build a better future, borrowing their name and symbols from the stonemasons of the Middle Ages.

Like alchemists, masons pursued a Great Work with God as the supreme architect.

More than a century later, in 1875, medium Helena Blavatsky co-founded the New York Theosophical Society. The society was based on principles of universal fraternity and promoted the comparative study of religions and the investigation of nature as a means of approaching the messages of occult masters and spiritual entities.

In the wake of this esoteric path—which was traversed by few, not because of discriminatory barriers but because it

was difficult and held little promise of success—some masons, again in England, founded the Golden Dawn, a Hermetic order based on an individual path in search of true knowledge. The Golden Dawn replaced the Theosophical Society's collective path to revelation with individual initiation, planting the seeds for many future solitary witches and wizards in contemporary society. The Irish poet William Butler Yeats belonged to this order, combining magic with the Celtic traditions of his homeland. His work was full of symbols, and could touch anyone with his descriptions of landscapes and images. For example, an abandoned tower, the moon, or a spiral staircase would represent uncertainty, destiny, and the spiral motion of life, even though they are all objects that exist in the world. This, after all, is the most authentic meaning of magic: not to produce the impossible, but to dive deeper into things, especially those that might seem lost.

It's a short step from the rebirth of wizards to the new face of witchcraft. This also took place in England, which is not surprising. One look at the witch trials shows that, although other countries on the continent had a higher number of victims, the English body of work on the subject, from essays to personal accounts, is astonishing. Nowhere else did witchcraft and magic raise such a debate written at the time of the persecutions. And to write is to remember, to plow the field. Thus, in the mid-20th century, esoteric priest Gerald Gardner introduced Wicca to the world and became its first priest.

Wicca was introduced as the ancient religion of European witches. This idea came from the influence of two books that are, unfortunately, historically inaccurate. The first, by Charles Leland, said that witchcraft derived directly from the goddess Diana, who had sent her daughter to the land of Aradia in order to teach the oppressed to fight back against their oppressors. The second, by Margaret Murray, explained that witchcraft was a relic of an ancient European cult that worshipped a horned god, the protector of vegetation.

In reality, witchcraft as a religion begins with Wicca, but these historically inaccurate sources created a poetic foundation for it. Although witchcraft was not a religion, it's nonetheless true that witches existed in every era, along with certain divine beings considered guardians of nature and the cosmos. Evidence of these is found in archaeological remains. Depictions of the Celtic god Cernunnos and the Divine Mother goddess are found in prehistoric statuettes, and they provided models for these contemporary practices.

Cernunnos is a hybrid god with long deer antlers, the lord and protector of beasts. The Mother Goddess, on the other hand, had enlarged sexual organs and womb to represent fertility, caregiving, and abundance. Both are nothing more than two manifestations of the Goddess and God found in contemporary rituals. They can be conjured either in modern gatherings or in solitude. Herbs, stones, spells, and objects that represent the elements are used in the rites. Alone or at gatherings, witches take part in a magic circle that represents the cycle of life, death, and rebirth.

Today, there are many forms of witchcraft that, along with Wicca, blend with neo-Pagan movements, which generally share their desire to be more in tune with nature.

One can be a witch or wizard even if one adheres to other religions or follows no specific spiritual aim. Wicca has various denominations, and other types of witchcraft favor different practices, such as herbs and plants, crystals, the ocean and water, fairies and other spiritual entities, or folklore and practices learned through studying or passed down by family. Witches and wizards might use shamanic and animistic traditions; follow complex rituals or simple daily acts, like cleaning a domestic space which has spiritual value; or believe in the divinities, myths, and beliefs of other religions around the world. There are fine lines between practices, one magical art blending with the next through personal awareness and intentions. Many witches are activists for human rights, the environment, animals, and minors. Even though activism is not an essential component, contemporary witches and wizards are undoubtedly dedicated to nature, which they don't perceive as an external entity but rather as a world we are part of.

More than anything, practicing magic today means working to develop a greater understanding of the essence of everything without turning a blind eye to darker things, like fear and death. Knowing that we live in a wonderful but unstable world is the first step towards living through justice, which means defending the weak—those who have no voice, or who cannot be heard by society. Magic is outward, an act of paying attention to the world, and inward, an act of taking care of our personal time and dreams. The Renaissance soul of the world has been reborn in our time, but has mixed with other religions and cultures, becoming fully open. It loses its exclusively human form and takes on a metamorphic, hybrid one in which humans, animals, plants, and spirits live together with equal dignity; in which the same responsibility is paid to others as to ourselves.

Through this attitude of respect, care, and equality for every form of life, the feminine aspect of the cosmos is often favored. We find that the image of the Triple Goddess—maiden, mother, and crone—corresponds to the three lunar phases of growth—waxing, full, and waning—as well as with enthusiasm, learning, and wisdom.

Nothing is left out. The witch knows that she must learn to live with joy as well as grief. She knows that she must be able to imagine positive things in the absence of good and remember the feeling of thirst even in moments of abundance.

Like the old witches of Thessaly, men and women who consider themselves wizards and witches evoke the moon by drawing it down at night. Let it be a strong moon—a moon that heralds courage.

∧ ∨ ∧ ∨ ∧

WITCHES
AND WIZARDS

Do witches and wizards really exist? We often associate them with fairy tales, myths, and sacred texts, and imagine them as ancient alchemists and rural healers. This chapter offers an overview of the witches and wizards from history and legend—cannibal witches, moon women, saints, wise wizards, poets, and blind fortune tellers, as well as versions of these from contemporary times.

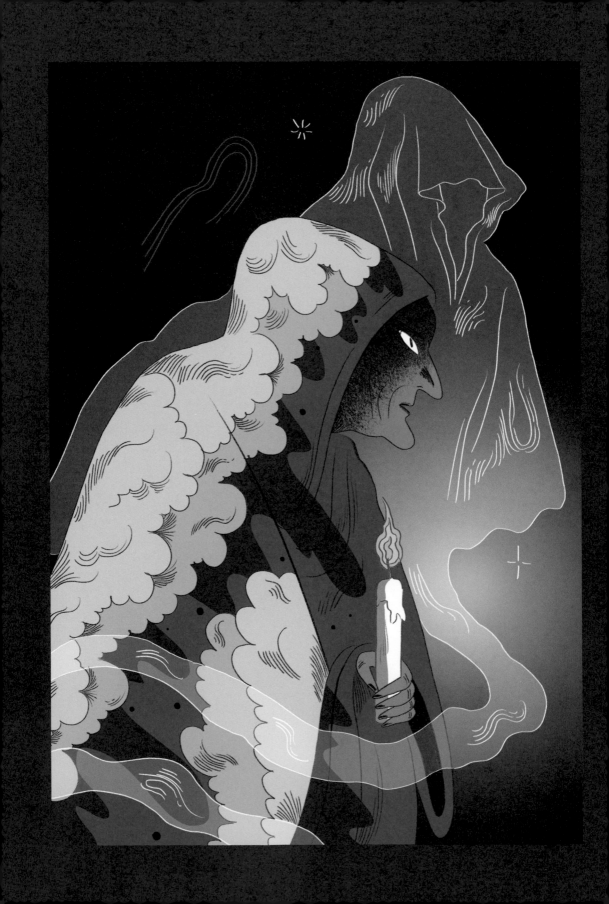

WITCH OF ENDOR

~ ~ ~

Necromancy is the art of conjuring the dead to question them about the fates of the living. Blind before an existence that no longer concerns them, the dead can peer within and beyond the soul to investigate the paths that lie before us. In the first book of the prophet Samuel, King Saul banned necromancers and magicians from Israel. However, during the war against the Philistines, after seeking the advice of God in vain through dreams, prophets, and divine oracles, he disguised himself and went to the city of Endor, where a necromancer lived. In the Rabbinic *Talmud*, this necromancer is identified as Zephaniah, the mother of Abner, cousin of the king and commander-in-chief of his army. Saul asks the woman to conjure the prophet Samuel, who had died shortly before and was buried in his native city. According to Jewish tradition, a person's ghost would float about the body for around a year before finally saying good-bye. When the ghost appeared, the witch became frightened, realizing that it was the king before her. However, he reassured her, saying "Don't be afraid! But what have you seen?" The woman replied to Saul "I have seen a divine being coming up from the ground!" He said to her "What about his appearance?" She said "An old man is coming up! He is wrapped in a robe!"

Unfortunately, the ghost of Samuel does not bring good news: Saul will be defeated, along with his entire army, because God has abandoned him. This event shows what happened as a result of Saul's action of consulting a fortune teller, which was against biblical law.

THE THREE WITCHES

~ ~ ~

"When shall we three meet again? / In thunder, lightning, or in rain?" the three witches from Shakespeare's *Macbeth* ask each other—a hint at their connection to the forces of weather and their role as harbingers of disaster. Old, androgynous, and wicked, the trio—three being a powerful number—represent the body, mind, and spirit; past, present, and future; birth, life, and death. They are ominous, representative of the vision from that time of those who perform magical arts, but they are also the descendants of other female trios from mythology who safeguard fate.

For example, there were the Scandinavian Norns, "those who whisper secrets" and lived near the well of fate, next to a tree that contained all the worlds. They sprayed the tree with well water every day; weaved the tapestry of lives on their loom, each thread a single person; and carved runes with the language of knowledge. The *Edda*, a book of poems of Norse mythology, says "They lay down laws. / They choose life / for the children of men, / speak destiny."

The Roman Parcae and Greek Moirai—in other words, the Fates—also weaved fates. In *Orlando Furioso*, Ariosto wrote: "Know that the Parcae are those ancient wives, / That in this fashion spin your feeble lives." Clotho spun the thread, overseeing birth; Lachesis decided how long it was; and Atropos cut it.

The three witches show parallels also in today's Triple Goddess symbol, representing the three lunar phases. For modern-day witches, this symbol depicts the three nocturnal phases of existence: waxing, full, and waning, which occur in cycles, in every person.

MORGAN LE FAY

Morgan le Fay is one of the most fascinating and mysterious figures from Arthurian legend and the vast folklore of witches. She embodies the ambiguity of the fay, or fairies, vague beings that linger at the edge of the living. They are capable of showing sincere kindness toward humans, or enduring hostility. In this form, she lives in the mysterious Avalon, "the isle of apples," which is often identified as the Tor above the English city of Glastonbury, a hill that sticks out like an island when the area floods. As a witch in human form, she is an expert in the healing arts. She is also King Arthur's half-sister and an apprentice to Merlin. At times, she is a fierce adversary of the Knights of the Round Table, and at others, she assists them. In any case, she is said to be the one who accompanies a fatally wounded Arthur on his final journey across the water to Avalon, where the king's body still lies today. Morgan's character also derives from her name, which is possibly based on the Celtic goddess Morrigan, who is associated with war and fate. Morrigan is a friend and enemy to the hero Cúchulainn, whose death she foretells. She is a goddess and spirit of Irish origin, and represents the ancestral power of her homeland. The name also recalls other creatures, like the Mari-Morgans, or Morgans, of Breton and Welsh mythology. These creatures contain both sexes and are experts in spells and secrets that come from the sea (*mori-gena*), similar to mermaids. They populate the depths of the sea, where they live a peaceful life. They often rescue victims from shipwrecks... but at other times cause the shipwreck themselves, acting on a whim.

 # BABA YAGA

~ ~ ~

Baba Yaga is a witch from Slavic folklore who roams in the depths of winter. There is nothing human about her, except for her appearance: an old witch with a hooked nose. If you look closer, her sneer reveals her iron teeth! The origins of her name are uncertain. In ancient Russian, *baba* was a sort of enchantress, whereas in modern Russian it is the root of the word for "grandmother". *Yaga*, however, is even more mysterious. It can be translated as "evil nymph" or as "snake." She lives in a hut called an *izba* that is said to stand on chicken legs or wheels and could open up onto this world or others. She flies while seated in a mortar, hunting children, and uses a broom to erase her tracks so no one knows when she has arrived or if she has left. She can control the wind and is associated with cold seasons.

A popular song about spring says "Sun, have you seen / the Old Yaga, / Baba Yaga, the witch of winter? / That fury, she ran away from spring, / ran away from its beauty, / she put the cold in a sack, / shook the cold from the Earth, / tripped and / rolled down the hill."

She is rather devious, putting heroes and heroines through difficult tests before helping them. But she is said to help those who are connected to her through mysterious bonds. Being mother and guardian of the forest, she must be somewhat of a mother (or grandmother) to us all. How might her *izba* welcome us when we arrive? What warning might she have in store for us—one of life, or one of death?

HECATE

Surely, at some point, you have stood at a crossroads, asking yourself if all roads are not the same, be it a crossroads in the countryside or one of destiny. Intersections are unique and powerful. In that place, all possible paths meet, and the result is our present.

Where life, death, and initiation into the mysteries meet, a triple-figure goddess illuminates the darkness with her two torches... or perhaps she is leading us farther into it. She is Hecate, the one with three bodies and the face of a dog, her animal familiar. She is an ancient goddess, more ancient than the Greco-Roman cults dedicated to her. When Persephone is kidnapped by Hades, god of the Underworld, Hecate hears her cries and warns Persephone's mother Demeter, goddess of the harvest. Alongside Demeter, she is the goddess of the mysteries of death and rebirth for the sanctuary of Eleusis. She is also connected to domestic altars, protecting against curses.

She might be a goddess of witches, but first and foremost she is a great asexual mother who can reproduce on her own. She is the goddess of births and wild creatures. She has three forms because she governs the earth, sea, and sky, and she moves freely between the worlds of humans, spirits, and gods. She holds the keys to the universe in her hands, and controls demons and the moon in its waning phase. Thanks to her, witches can conjure the dead, see ghosts, and cast spells.

Offerings of food and aromas, like orzo, sweets and honey, and asphodel flowers, were left at crossroads for Hecate, dark divinities, and the restless dead.

MATTEUCCIA DA TODI

~ ~ ~

Love potions. That was one of the 30 charges that led Matteuccia di Francesco to be sentenced to death by burning at the stake by the Todi court of witchcraft on March 20, 1428. "Witch doctor," "woman of ill repute," and "witch" were some of the words used to describe her. Some of the ingredients she used were wax, herbs, and the powder of burned swallows to attract or repulse the attention of men or placate a violent husband, and the fat of cadavers to invoke the name of Christ, the Virgin Mary, and the saints, the most powerful beings imaginable.

In the past, Catholic miracles and magic were intertwined, but for the judges, any spell was the work of Satan. Matteuccia was one of the first victims of the witch hunts in Europe and perhaps also the first to describe what took place at demonic Sabbaths.

The trial documents say that she covered herself with some ointment made from the blood of nocturnal birds and killed newborns so that she could reach the walnut tree of Benevento, where many other witches gathered around Lucifer in person.

"Unguent, unguent, / send me to the walnut tree of Benevento, / Under the water and under the wind, / under all bad weather."

The Devil himself, fully incarnate, sent her a demon in the form of a goat so that she could ride it to the gathering spot. "Oh Lucibello, / demon from hell, / because you were banned, / you changed / your name to Lucifer the most powerful, / come to me or send one of your servants."

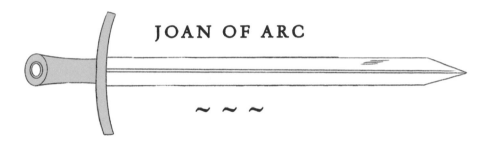

JOAN OF ARC

~ ~ ~

Why is Joan of Arc, the patron saint of France, remembered as a witch? It all began one summer in her native town of Domrémy when the 13-year-old Joan heard spiritual voices that she identified as the archangel Michael and the saints Catherine and Margaret. From that moment on, she decided that she would devote herself to God and took a vow of chastity. Meanwhile, the French were fighting England and Burgundy in the Hundred Years War. In the autumn of 1428, Joan departed to save the dauphin, the rightful future king, as the voices had instructed her to do.

She did not surrender when the captains at arms thought she was mad. The people already admired her charisma, which prevailed in the end. Joan met Charles VII after passing the ecclesiastical interrogations and revealing details about him that no one could have known except through divine intervention. She went to war on horseback with a sword and white standard, instilling courage in her soldiers. She led the army to triumph in the battle of Orléans, and in 1429 she attended the coronation of the king at the cathedral in Reims.

But such a tenacious and transparent woman was unpopular with those in power. She could have bewitched them with the truth. In 1431, she was captured by enemies and condemned to death by burning at the stake in Rouen. She was 19 years old. The trial came to be considered illegal just a few years later. Those in power feared her strength, her masculinity, and the candor of her conviction. Using religion as an excuse, her trial was a vile political campaign that aimed to destabilize the new French kingdom by persecuting its most ardent visionary.

URSULA KEMP

~ ~ ~

Ursula Kemp, also known as Grey, was one of 14 women tried for witchcraft in the village of Saint Osyth in the county of Essex. She was accused of having killed a child she had initially cured and was condemned to death by hanging in 1582 at 57 years old. As in many other cases, she embodied a combination of wise woman and witch. She in fact confessed to having learned magic from another woman who had given her a remedy for lameness, which had been caused by a curse. This remedy contained Saint John's wort, chervil, pig manure, and sage. The first case of a familiar, the animal companions of English witches that sucked the blood of their human, is found in documents about her trial. Thomas Rabbet, the woman's eight-year-old son, who was coerced by the judge, gave witness to Ursula's true nature and her familiars. She had four familiars, which had comforting names and domestic appearances but demonic habits: Titty, a grey cat; Tiffin, a white lamb; Piggin, a black female toad; and Jack, a black cat that "would suck the blood from his mother's arms and other parts of her body at night." Ursula explained that the two male familiars punished by killing, whereas the female ones crippled and made people and livestock sick.

    In 1921, two female skeletons were discovered near Saint Osyth. They had iron nails in their knees and elbows, a method used to prevent witches from rising from the dead. They are believed to be Ursula, and Elizabeth Bennet, another witch.

BIDDY EARLY

~ ~ ~

Some witches are known for their wisdom. "The wisest of wise women" was how poet William Butler Yeats described Irish woman Biddy Early (1798–1872), who lived in County Clare. She was an herbalist, healer, and clairvoyant. She was so famous that people came from all across Ireland to see her and receive cures of the mind and body for humans and animals. She was born Bridget Connors, but she rejected her father's surname, along with those of the four husbands she outlived, and adopted that of her mother, whose powers she inherited. As a girl, she spent seven years with the "Good People," or the fairies, as an apprentice—because the fairies, Biddy said, needed to share their secrets. Moreover, perhaps due to their nostalgic, sometimes human-like nature, fairies have a weakness for orphans, which Biddy was. She had to learn to get by, developing a proud and untamable personality, which helped her to face bullies and those who accused her of witchcraft, especially priests. Through her gifts and nature, she gained the support of many people, who defended her when she was tried in 1865. Even several accusers recanted their charges.

One object she was known for was a blue bottle, which she used to collect herbs, dew (which transformed night into dawn), water from her magic well, and holy water. The bottle was said to have come from her dead son Paddy, who had won it in a competition with the fairies and then returned to life to give it to her.

MARIE CATHERINE LAVEAU

~ ~ ~

Marie Catherine Laveau (1801–1881), the New Orleans queen of Voodoo, was a Creole woman whose story is intertwined with myth. In Louisiana, the Voodoo tradition combined Catholic elements with the Voodoo spiritual universe, where the Loa lived. The Loa were intermediaries between God and humans. Marie Laveau was the daughter of a freed slave and a Creole businessman. She was a devout Catholic her entire life. In the collective imagination, she became both something of a saint and a terrifying, deceiving witch. She performed healings with spells and herbal potions, was an expert in love magic, and could predict her future. Everyone apparently went to her in search of advice. Her obituary in the *New York Times* read "Lawyers, legislators, planters, merchants all came to pay their respects to her and seek her offices."

But Marie Laveau was much more than a simple urban witch doctor. Her second marriage was to a white man, Christopher Glapion, with whom she had many children. Some came down with yellow fever, which was ravaging the city at that time. Because of this, she dedicated herself to the sick and weak, developing her magical talents.

What's real, and what's legend? The stories of Marie Laveau that we find in novels and personal accounts reflect more on her fame than on questioning the facts. This happens with true witches. They disappear, but their magic remains—especially if, as in the case of Laveau, their magic inspires freedom at a time of slavery and racism.

HELENA PETROVNA BLAVATSKY

~ ~ ~

East and West converge in the figure of Helena Petrovna Blavatsky (1831–1891), founder of the Theosophic Society and a woman devoted to studying divine knowledge. She was born in Dnipro, Ukraine, and died of the flu in London. The events of her life made her the mother of modern magic, as she embodied its potential and ambiguity. Her gifts as a medium created an oracular aura around her, but also gave her the reputation of a charlatan. Her imagination "held the folklore of the entire world," wrote Yeats.

She was lively and kind, but full of incoherent theories that cast doubts on the reliability of her work. As part of an aristocratic family, she traveled extensively as a child and developed an interest in esotericism that she taught herself. She received her psychic powers from the Mahatma, spiritual masters she met in India, superior beings who had ascended from the human to the divine by way of various initiations. The diverse body of work she left behind is a sometimes confusing, but always fascinating mix of ancient writers and philosophers and Indian and Mediterranean traditions in which the voice of the author blends with the knowledge of the past and other places. This, however, stirred accusations of plagiarism from her fiercest critics. For Blavatsky, her work was considerably less important than what came from it: a universal fraternity of human spirit.

Madame Blavatsky believed that humanity would shift from a materialistic culture to a purely spiritual one before the start of the new century. Although this didn't happen, she planted a colorful seed that could still perhaps blossom into something unexpected.

STARHAWK

~ ~ ~

If you were to find a common denominator among all witches and their fates throughout history, it would be their charisma. This was their shining inner strength, which transformed them into healers, enemies of society, and inspiring figures. For the American Starhawk (1951), this charisma is fused with environmentalism, pacifism, and feminism. She was a lone witch for years until she founded two congregations for women in the San Francisco Bay Area: Compost, and Honeysuckle. In the 1970s, Starhawk, along with Diane Baker, brought to life the practice of "reclaiming," a magical tradition based on a dialogue between the Goddess religion and the fight for minorities, gender equality, and the environment.

Not all modern-day witches are so politically active, and some view activism with suspicion. However, Starhawk's first act of magic was that she gave a voice to the earth, the oppressed, and the dream of a community in which diversity is valued, not a cause for marginalization.

In her most important book, *The Spiral Dance*, she writes "Love for life in all its forms is the basic ethic of Witchcraft." This love recognizes the destructive and regenerative forces of the cosmos and doesn't hide from the shadow of existence. This love puts justice first, justice that "is administered by some external authority based on a written code or set of rules imposed from without. Instead, justice is an inner sense that each act brings about consequences that must be faced responsibly."

TIRESIAS

~ ~ ~

"See Tiresias, who changed his likeness / when he was turned from male to female, / transformed in every member. / Later on he had to touch once more / the two twined serpents with his rod / before he could regain his manly plumes." Dante wrote of the Theban clairvoyant in canto 20 of the *Inferno*, the canto of the diviners, whose heads were turned backwards in eternal punishment for their desire to look too far ahead when they were alive. There are many stories about how Tiresias lost their sight, which gave them prophetic gifts. The one in the quote above comes from Ovid's *Metamorphosis*, and says that Tiresias had hit two serpents with a stick while they were mating and because of this was turned into a woman. After seven years, they encountered the snakes again and once more hit them and returned to their male form. Therefore, Tiresias was familiar with the natures of both females and males. They were thus called upon to settle an argument between the father of the gods, Zeus, and his wife, Hera, about whether women or men experience more pleasure. Tiresias agreed with Zeus, saying that it was, without a doubt, women. Offended, Hera blinded them, but Zeus in return gave them foresight.

In the *Odyssey*, Homer's Odysseus meets Tiresias, who lives in the Underworld, where the hero has gone to seek advice from the enchantress Circe. Tiresias predicts his destiny but also implies that he always has free choice, even when the gods are opposed to him. Therefore, Tiresias, the blind person, just like the author Homer, sees not only events that will unravel, but also the qualities of those who question them. They see beyond because they can peruse the human soul.

MERLIN

~ ~ ~

The figure of Merlin comes from 12th-century Britain and Wales, and is a combination of various characters: a prophet, a bard, a mad hermit. Stories claim he was the son of a woman and a demon, and that he had the gift of foresight. The wisdom of old age, that of one who has lived many lives (perhaps due to his demon ancestry), hides within him as a child.

As a boy, Merlin revealed to King Vortigern that the king's attempt to build a tower on a certain piece of land was destined for failure because below it stood the battleground of the Red and White Dragon, which represented future conflict within the kingdom. Merlin was also the cause of the birth of the legendary King Arthur. He used his magic to allow the new British king, Uther Pendragon, to spend a night with Igraine, the wife of his enemy, the Duke of Cornwall, resulting in the birth of Arthur. 18th-century poet Alfred Tennyson says that it was Merlin himself who saved a newborn Arthur upon the death of the king, extracting him from the waves of the sea and giving him shelter in a cave under the castle of Tintagel, which still exists today and can be visited.

What happened to the wise and demonic Merlin? According to the most well-known legend, his student Viviane, in an attempt to defend herself from her master's inappropriate attention, imprisoned him forever in the enchanted forest of Brocéliande. Merlin is said to still roam inside what he believes is a glass tower, but passersby claim to see a cloud in the shape of the wizard's face.

NICOLAS FLAMEL

~ ~ ~

Was there really someone who could turn base metal into gold? This was the case with the mysterious French alchemist Nicolas Flamel, whose story blends history and fairy tale. After all, little was actually known about the alchemists, whose lives were sealed away and protected by secrecy, inseparable from their work. Born in 1330, Flamel lived in Paris with his wife Perenelle. He owned two shops where he carried out his work as a scribe. He eventually became known for his frequent donations to the church. He died in 1418, but some believe he is still alive today due to his discovery of the philosopher's stone, which can heal anything, and therefore cure illnesses and elude death. Writings about him mainly come from 17th-century texts. The story of his alchemical knowledge follows a classic story of magic in which a book, a journey, and a foreigner meet. Flamel bought a grimoire for a few cents and with it went to Spain, where he sought help translating its language and symbols from a Jewish converso. His story is largely invented. Flamel's wealth comes from the inheritance his wife received after the death of her first husband. Or perhaps the philosopher's stone is nothing but a seed of one's fantasy, and when it is associated with a name on a tombstone, it puts down roots and begins to stretch from mind to mind by way of its golden—or magical—branches.

MARSILIO FICINO

~ ~ ~

"All nature is a magician," Marsilio Ficino wrote in his book *De Vita Libri Tres*. The Renaissance philosopher, astrologer, and humanist was the son of Cosimo de' Medici's personal physician. He translated Plato's work into Latin and founded the Florence Platonic Academy, a place where intellectuals of that time met to exchange ideas. But the true academy that Ficino imagined unfurled across centuries. He believed that there was a continuity between ancient philosophy and Christian doctrine. This knowledge, which passed through philosophy and religion, had to do with the soul as a mediator between the body and the divine; between decomposition and eternity.

Drawing on an ancient concept, Ficino saw the cosmos as a living being connected to the divine through the bonds of love. Magic was the art that investigated that concept, descending and ascending the ladder of beings, from matter to the spirit, from stones and plants to animals, humans, the heavens, angels, and God. To him, there were two types of magic: natural magic, which helped stabilize relations between medicine and astrology by studying how celestial bodies influence health and human character; and demonic, evil magic, which involved diviner rituals and the conjuring of demons to increase one's individual power.

When Ficino was accused of practicing magic against religion, he defended himself with the evangelical example of the Magi, who were the first to visit Jesus, and explained that magic was a means of nurturing the world, knowing it and drawing nourishment from it by finding connections between big and small things.

PARACELSUS

~ ~ ~

Theophrastus von Hohenheim, known as Paracelsus (1493–1541), was a Swiss physician, humanist, and philosopher from the Renaissance era. But why is he also remembered as a magician who went on to inspire Goethe's *Faust*?

Paracelsus can be considered enlightened for many reasons. He invented iatrochemistry, an art that led to modern pharmacology. He formulated the idea that diseases could be attacked and destroyed by certain medicines, and that well-being did not depend solely on the balance of bodily fluids and blood as had been believed since antiquity. He is credited with the discovery of the chemical element zinc, and the use of essences and tinctures that derive from plants and mineral compositions.

When he was accused of using poison, he claimed that everything had some poisonous qualities but it was the dosage that made it a poisonous substance. His work was fundamentally alchemical, and that's why he earned the reputation of a magician. He turned the alchemist's famous search for gold into a search for new medicinal methods to promote health and long life, jumping from science to magic like many of his peers. Nonetheless, magic was the first form of science, and it brings a highly spiritual element to science, showing that everything is connected. To paraphrase Paracelsus himself, humans are nothing more than a microcosm that reflects the macrocosm they live in; therefore, wisdom and healing don't derive only from the study of diseases, but also from understanding the relationships between living beings in the vast secrets of the universe.

JOHN DEE

~ ~ ~

Often when we imagine a magician, we see a man lost in his books in a room full of mysterious objects, illuminated by twilight. The magician in this image is similar to what John Dee (1527–1608) must have looked like in his vast library in London. The story of Dee, who was an astronomer, mathematician, antiquarian, adviser to Queen Elizabeth I, cartographer, and occultist, is a story about the search for knowledge, and a story of failure.

The versatility and variety of the arts the magician studied were equal to the misfortune of his ventures. He was a respected scientist who decided to turn his studies to the world of spirits, searching for superior powers that could finally solve the mystery of the philosopher's stone that medieval alchemists had pursued. There was a fine line between science and magic. While both aimed to reveal what was hidden in nature, only magic was a means of penetrating the spiritual world... even if it meant the risk of losing oneself.

Included among the magical objects he probably possessed were a crystal ball and an obsidian mirror, objects that couldn't reflect this world and therefore faced the other one. When he was accused of witchcraft, Dee defended himself by explaining that the only beings he listened to were angels. The advice of angels, however, didn't help him in this life. Erudition often goes hand in hand with naivety, and Dee placed his trust in charlatans like Edward Kelley, who was a medium as well as a criminal and con artist. Dee's vast knowledge always managed to earn him admiration, but it did not help him economically. He died in poverty after selling all his incredible books.

GIORDANO BRUNO

~ ~ ~

The year 1600 began with one of the most memorable and atrocious burnings at the stake from that time period. On February 17, in Rome's Campo de' Fiori, the philosopher Giordano Bruno was burned for heresy. A defense for the free search for truth against the abuses of power burned with him.

As he was forced to kneel for his sentence, he said "Perhaps you pronounce this sentence against me with greater fear than I receive it." Born in Nola in 1548, Bruno was a Dominican monk, but his philosophy incorporated many mysterious teachings. He was a radical reformist who distinguished between official religion, which helped control the masses, and esoteric religion, which allowed a few curious people to study the nature of the universe and the divine. In his philosophical school of thought, Bruno preferred the paganism of the ancient world to Christian elements. Some of the objects he used in his work were plants and stones, as well as a series of talismans to draw on the benefits of the stars. He was a follower of Copernican theories, which believed that the sun was the center of our galaxy. Bruno went beyond this, though, and imagined the plurality of worlds. The universe was full of vital power, and God wasn't so much its creator as he was its highest form. This pantheistic view stripped humans and the earth of their dominance and gave it to the universe, believed to be alive, eternal, and infinite. Magic was a tool used to mediate rational thought and the imagination.

The universal knowledge that Bruno pursued was the first notion of the possibility that life existed elsewhere in space beyond our planet.

PROSPERO

~ ~ ~

Magic is art, deceit, and performance. We are reminded of this by the sorcerer Prospero from *The Tempest* (1611), Shakespeare's final play, in which the character is the Bard's alter ego. Prospero is the creator of the events that occur in the play. He controls, imprisons, then redeems destinies before his own redemption. He was the rightful Duke of Milan until his brother Antonio usurped him and exiled him to an island in the Mediterranean with his daughter Miranda. Twelve years pass, like the months in a year. On the island, he meets extraordinary creatures, like the monster Caliban—a fish-human and son of a witch who has trapped Ariel, an air spirit, in a tree. After Caliban tries to rape Miranda, Prospero makes him a slave, and Ariel, once free of the tree, becomes Prospero's faithful servant. When a ship carrying Prospero's usurper brother Antonio, King of Naples, and his son Ferdinand, passes near the coast, Prospero unleashes the elements and causes a shipwreck. Misunderstandings, illusions, Miranda and Ferdinand falling in love, and the unmasking of Antonio follow. Eventually, they prepare to return to Milan. Ariel once again becomes wind without a master.

The will of the sorcerer steers everything. Taking his leave from the stage, Prospero says "Ye all which it inherit, shall dissolve / And, like this insubstantial pageant faded, / Leave not a rack behind. We are such stuff / As dreams are made on, and our little life / Is rounded with a sleep."

Our dreaming is a spell that suspends lives within time, like islands in the sea, making them seem eternal.

WILLIAM BLAKE

~ ~ ~

"The tree which moves some to tears of joy is in the eyes of others only a green thing which stands in the way. Some see nature all ridicule and deformity, and by these I shall not regulate my proportions; and some scarce see nature at all. But to the eyes of the man of imagination, nature is imagination itself," wrote William Blake (1757–1827) in a letter.

The poet, painter, and visionary Blake spent his life in London in poverty, without recognition. In his work, it is his spirit that speaks as it explores the living world, recognizing that it is full of revelations, and viewing the details of it as its grandeur. Blake is both an artist who describes a garden funeral for fairies the size of grasshoppers, and who rants about the oppression of institutional religion.

Ever since he was a child, Blake had visions of angels and supernatural beings, which for some made him a madman but for others made him a mystic. There is a fine line between the two. A mystic seeks contact with the divine, undergoing an initiation process, which for Blake was the purpose of poetry, in verse and visual form. The specular forces of innocence and experience derive from the divine, whereas humans have the power to dream beyond the constraints of any system.

In the caption of his painting of Newton, bent foolishly over his instruments and surrounded by darkness, Blake writes "He who sees the Infinite in all things sees God. He who sees the Ratio only sees himself only." Where science defines the borders of a prison-universe, art dissolves them. Art is the true philosopher's stone, acting through poetic imagination. And thus magic can, in the words of Blake, "open eternal worlds."

ALEISTER CROWLEY

The year the Theosophical Society was founded is the year the controversial figure Aleister Crowley (1875–1947) was born. Crowley was scandalous, transgressive, and satanic. He was portrayed in the newspapers as a negative magician for his drug abuse, sexual tendencies—he was openly bisexual—and the satanic inspiration of the name he gave himself, "the Beast 666." However, Crowley didn't believe in either the Christian God or the Devil. He professed the power of individual will, and magic was an expression of that, used to navigate the world.

His rebellion against conformity is seen in his choice of name. He was born Edward Alexander, but during his years at Cambridge he changed it to Aleister, the Gaelic version of Alexander and an homage to the poem *Alastor, or The Spirit of Solitude* by Romantic poet Percy Bysshe Shelley. He was a member of the Golden Dawn, then a leader of the magical religious order O.T.O (Ordo Templi Orientis). In the 1920s, he founded his own spiritual commune, the Abbey of Thelema ("will" in Greek), in Cefalù, Sicily. In addition to ceremonial magic, which allowed contact with supernatural beings, sexual magic was also prominent. He was banned for this, but to Crowley, sexual transgression was an ecstatic act that could push the mind beyond its narrow limits through bodily excess.

A magician was anyone who dared to cross the borders between the pure and impure, madness and reason, freeing themselves with the same power contained in a star because, Crowley wrote, "Every man and every woman is a star." He lived the rest of his life in England, bankrupt and miserable.

GERALD GARDNER

~ ~ ~

Witchcraft today is a religion recognized by many countries, thanks to Gerald Gardner (1884–1964), who, in the mid-19th century, made Wicca an official religion. He was born to a well-off family, and, because of an illness, spent much of his childhood in warmer countries. Therefore, he had no traditional education. He was self-taught, and as an adult was passionate about anthropology and archaeology. When he returned to England in the 1930s, Gardner moved to the county of Dorset, where he adopted the practice of witchcraft after meeting the coven of witches of the New Forest. He was likely initiated by the priestess Dafo, or Edith Rose Woodford-Grimes, at Mill House, which belonged to Dorothy Clutterbuck, or "Old Dorothy," who was outwardly conservative, hiding her true devotion to nature.

Gardner described the coven as a group initially founded by blood relatives, clarifying that witchcraft is hereditary. He might not have been the founder of Wicca, but he is credited with its dissemination. He developed the Wheel of the Year calendar based on eight events and seasonal holidays, and the set of rites and instructions reworked from various sources, today known as "Gardnerian Wicca." In magical terms, Gardner's character evokes that of a trickster, a big con artist of myths, a fascinating liar able to get by in any situation. But let's not forget that in many cultures, the trickster is the one who obtained fire for humanity, not because they invented it but because they stole it with their wits from the gods and brought it to our world.

GANDALF

~ ~ ~

The wizard Gandalf is a character from Middle Earth in *The Lord of the Rings* and other books by J.R.R. Tolkien. He belongs to the race of wizards and wears the Ring of Fire, Narya, one of the three Elven rings that were not forged by the Dark Lord Sauron and therefore not bound to his will.

The creatures of Middle Earth turn to Gandalf for advice. He is not an old wizard locked in his tower. He uses his staff as a weapon, rides his noble Shadowfax, and is a friend of the eagles. He initially wears the clothes of the Grey Pilgrim along with a wide-brimmed and pointy blue hat, traveling the various regions to get to know the inhabitants of even the most isolated places, like the Hobbits, who live peacefully in the Shire, ignorant of the world's torments. The wizard knows that even modest creatures have hidden power that can prove redemptive.

Gandalf undergoes a complete transformation and becomes Gandalf the White after fighting against the powers of fire in the form of the monster Balrog, falling into the abyss, and being reborn with renewed purity. Aspects of Gandalf recall the Norse god Odin, father of the Æsir, who often disguises himself among humans in the form of an anonymous wanderer. The wizard is superhuman, but his body makes him subject to the whims of the living, which recalls the figure of Christ, finding redemption in humans by experiencing their fragility.

INSTRUMENTS

Every witch and wizard worthy of the name has secrets and an imaginary bag where they keep them. These secrets can be objects: books, artifacts and tokens, gifts and inherited pieces, or the most powerful instrument of all—themselves. This chapter presents some of the most common magical objects used, as well as sharing historical examples and some instructions for use.

THE BODY

. : .

Body parts, from hair and nails to fluids, have frequently been used for spells and potions. The bodies of condemned witches from the witch hunt period showed presumed signs of satanic alliance left by the Devil himself. Today, magic has distanced itself from this old idea of demonization and is more focused on how to take care of the body, it being our primary resource. The balance we often pursue largely coincides with achieving harmony with our entire body. Many witches and wizards prefer to work *skyclad*, or naked, believing nudity to be the best way to contact divinities and nature, which our bodies are an expression of. With the passing of time, the story in our skin, our flesh, and our bones is enriched, even if it seems like our movements, liveliness, and beauty begin to betray us. They actually don't. They simply change. Being aware of this means understanding the power of the body because it does not reject any of its manifestations, nor does it find them embarrassing and useless. The female body is an example of this because it goes through so many transformations. It creates life and is familiar with separation and the cyclical nature of birth, deterioration, and death. Every age has its own specific magic. Childhood and adolescence have energetic, abundant, and fluid magic in the blood. In old age, it lives in the bones, the home of the soul, where bodies communicate with ancestors and prepare to cross the final threshold.

THE MIND

. : .

In the dark age of witchcraft, between the late Middle Ages and the early modern period, the mind was where one experienced the Devil's illusions. Many doubted the effective powers of witches, but no one questioned the acts of the Devil against Christianity. Skeptics didn't believe in their curses, but they did believe they could manipulate weak and easily influenced minds—often those of women and the elderly—with satanic forces. Their errors and faults were found in this mental weakness, which was subjugated by diabolical tricks. Evil spirits that sneaked into the imagination at night and returned from tainted bodily fluids with strange vapors were considered responsible for nightmares and visions. Body and mind were united by a fluid, permeable relationship that was subject to the influence of external influences that took advantage of the fragility caused by sickness or physical illness. Freeing ourselves of the idea of a devil that influences us, we give the mind independence, which fosters concentration, dreams, imagination, words, and communication. From concentration, we gain focus; from dreams, we get unique and revealing perspectives; from imagination, a new view of the world; from words, spells and conjuring, which communicate our intentions; and from communication, the meeting of the invisible with the visible. Our mind feeds our illusions and dispels them. It can both lead us off the beaten path and help us find ourselves, perhaps because to truly understand what path we are on, we must lose ourselves. Even getting lost, as in a fairy tale, can spark something magical.

THE GRIMOIRE

· : ·

Those who keep a diary know how much power is contained in those pages, even when a memory has faded or thoughts seem to belong to another life. The grimoire, the name of which comes from the medieval French *gramaire*, or "grammar book," is like a special diary. It is a rulebook for the occult arts. Some witches and wizards have one that they update and modify over time; others accumulate many, each with a different focus. They write down spells, summonings, and seals, instructions for creating amulets and potions, and natural and supernatural secrets. It contains all their magical knowledge—both what they've taught and what they've learned. From antiquity to today, such books have been strictly handwritten, bearing the individual's personal imprint and instilling effectiveness in the words through writing. One of the most famous and oldest grimoires is the *Clavicula Salomonis* (*The Key of Solomon*), attributed to King Solomon from the Bible. It was assembled in the Middle East and then spread to Europe before it was banned by the Inquisition in 1559. Like any powerful object, it survived, and less than a century later the first printed copy appeared in Rome. The latest evolution of the grimoire is the *Book of Shadows*. First created by Gerald Gardner for his Wicca rituals, it eventually became a generic magic book for various neopagan traditions.

Made out of a crooked branch and inscribed with mysterious symbols, the wand is synonymous with witchcraft, like a staff for a wizard, which can become a possible enchanted weapon when necessary. Staffs and wands were used by ancient gods and prophetic figures. In the biblical Book of Exodus, Moses carried a sacred staff that was blessed by the Jewish God, which he used to defeat the wizards of the Egyptian pharaoh. In Greek mythology, the god Hermes had a staff called the Caduceus, formed by two intertwining snakes. The enchantress Circe used a wand, as did the goddess Athena, which she used to transform Odysseus into an old man. Medieval grimoires contained images of scepters, staffs, and wands as special magical objects. A wand can be made of glass, metal, crystal or gemstone, or wood, the most common material, is used to direct one's focus when casting spells. A unique bond is established between the individual and the instrument. That's why it's important not only to choose one with care but also, if possible, to make it from a fallen branch or one that has been pushed ashore by the current. Wands have a shaft and a point, a positive and a negative end, which can be used for different purposes. Powerful wands are made of alder, oak, or walnut, beech, holly, silver, or selenite. One made from a service tree is perfect for protection; one from an apple tree is for love; a gold one is for defense and prosperity; a hawthorn wand is used to communicate with fairies; and a lavender and willow wand is good for healing.

THE CHALICE

· ⁚ ·

The water of existence courses through the chalice, a cup that represents the heart, feeling, and intuition. We draw from the chalice in order to achieve intimate contact with things, to understand them from within before acting on them. It can contain water, wine, or some other drink that can be shared with ancestors, gods, ritual companions, or parts of ourselves we wish to speak with. It can also represent the union of the female and male principles when mixed with the wand or knife, but more importantly, this combination manifests the values of alliance and reconciliation. The chalice can be made of metal, wood, or terracotta. It can be a cup or a decorative instrument. Sometimes a horn or large shell, a symbol of sea energy, is used in place of the chalice. In Christian tradition, the chalice contains Jesus' blood, which is drunk by believers to spiritually cleanse and protect themselves. One of the most famous chalices is the Holy Grail, the ancient magical chalice of life that is later reimagined from a Christian perspective. According to religious legends, the Grail was the cup that Jesus drank from at the Last Supper, and Joseph of Arimathea, who was tasked with burying Jesus after the crucifixion, collected his blood in it. This chalice appears also in Arthurian legend. The mysterious cup heals the king and land, which are inextricably connected. To drink from the chalice is to drink from the spring of spiritual life. It is an act of celebration. With magic, every small thing echoes throughout the soul, and the soul feeds on such simple gestures.

THE CAULDRON

. : .

Witches and wizards mix potions, prepare elixirs, and sometimes cook soups full of herbs in their cauldrons. They can draw from the cauldron by sipping powerful concoctions, or they can enter the cauldron and let the magic do the rest so that they emerge renewed. It is a symbol of abundance, prosperity, and, more importantly, rebirth. In ancient mythology, heroes and gods came out of cauldrons stronger than before. Welsh mythology had the Pair Dadeni, the Cauldron of Rebirth, which was given to King Bran by a couple of giants who had escaped Ireland. The Welsh enchantress Ceridwen brews her elixir of wisdom and poetic inspiration in her cauldron. In a particularly shamanic Greek myth, a young Dionysus is torn to pieces by the Titans, boiled in a cauldron, and eaten. Zeus, however, uses his heart, the only part of him left, to completely regenerate him in divine form. From mythology to archaeology, the most fascinating cauldron has to be the silver cauldron of Gundestrup from the 2nd century BCE, which was found in a peat bog near the Danish village of the same name. However, it had been forged elsewhere, perhaps near the Danube. The relief work shows various Celtic gods, including Cernunnos, the horned god of nature. Finally, we have the Slavic fable of the frightening Baba Yaga, who flies around while seated in a cauldron! The cauldron of modern-day witches, often present on altars in smaller forms, is mainly used to burn incense and herbs or to offer drinks and other substances.

THE KNIFE

. : .

There are many types of knives used by witches and wizards
for various reasons. A knife can be a tool for cutting up herbs
and carving symbols and designs on wands, candles, or other
instruments; or it can be a ceremonial blade, which is called
an "athame" for many modern-day witches. The latter has
a double-edged blade and a black handle. It is consecrated
during a waning moon. The ceremonial blade is used to
direct and distance the flow of energy. The word "athame"
was first used by Gerald Gardner, but it seems to have come
from something similar found in the Renaissance-era grimoire
The Key of Solomon, a word that comes from the Latin
artavus, which means small knife or pocket knife. The ritual
use of the blade is ancient. Knives that weren't used for cutting
were discovered in Egyptian tombs. Knives made of bone were
found in the Grotte de la Vache in southern France. They are
believed to have been used for religious purposes 15,000 years
ago. Flint arrowheads from the prehistoric age have assumed
magical significance over time, becoming daggers of fate. The
blade is a symbol of clarity and purification. These recall the
shining blade of Excalibur, the sword of wisdom and truth
from Arthurian legend, which was guarded by the Lady of the
Lake. An enlightening newer version of the enchanted blade is
the Subtle Knife, an object from the second book of the same
name in Philip Pullman's *His Dark Materials trilogy.* This
knife chooses the bearer, has the power to cut any surface, and
can open windows between worlds.

THE PENTACLE

. : .

The value of our talismans is subject to many factors, like where and from whom they derive, what they represent, how we chose or found them, and what they are made of. In the grimoire *The Key of Solomon*, the word used for talisman is "pentacle," which refers to a variety of symbols, names, and letters that are inscribed within a circle, evoking the power of the elements contained in the universe: earth, water, fire, air, and aether (or spirit). It can be drawn on paper or parchment, carved in clay or wood, depicted on a metal amulet, or arranged out of crystals, herbs, or cloth. It can also be sewn or embroidered on clothes, placed on an altar, or hung on a wall. The five realms meet in the highly protective symbol, reminding us that what exists outside of us also exists within us. Anything that moves in the universe has the same intense effect on the body and mind of each individual. If we draw parallels between the symbol and the beliefs of ancient medicine, we also find that the elements match up with the four bodily humors that regulate the psychophysical balance of humans, as well as the four ages of man. Air is blood and childhood; fire is yellow bile and youth; water is phlegm and maturity; earth is black bile and old age. Lastly, aether, or universal spirit, is the individual soul. The upper point of the star refers to the ascensional and purgative journey of the spirit through matter.

THE HAT

. : .

You could recognize a witch or wizard by the fact that they dress however they like, according to their personality, whether it be a suit and tie or a rainbow-colored overcoat. Clothing is an expression of self. It doesn't matter if one rejects conformity or follows the latest trends. However, there is one piece of clothing that immediately comes to mind when we think of the magical arts: the pointed hat. There are two hypotheses as to the origins of this unique type of hat. The first is that it came from the hat that Jewish people in 13th century Europe were forced to wear for identification. Hatred toward Jews was sadly common. In the Middle Ages, many of the devilish characteristics attributed to them converged with magical stereotypes. The other hypothesis arrives a few centuries later in England with the conical, wide-brimmed black hat of Quakers, a Christian movement founded in 1652. The Quakers preached social equality and rejected hierarchy. It's not surprising, then, that their ideas were often considered heretical! Finally, we have the film adaptation of L. Frank Baum's *The Wizard of Oz*, in which the Wicked Witch of the West wears a pointed black hat. According to one fable, ancient English witches would put on their hats and go wherever they liked, usually to the village wine cellars to empty them out undisturbed! I like to think of the hat as a place where you can hide a wand, let a tired robin rest, or even hold a nest for warmth.

THE ALTAR

. : .

The altar is a sacred space dedicated to meditation, prayer, and spells. It can be placed in any part of the home: on the floor, a dresser, a table, or a bookshelf, or it can be placed outside, in a garden or courtyard. You can also make many altars depending on your needs and imagination. Witches and wizards are generally very good at this. They can be temporary or permanent, and there are various types. There's the seasonal altar, which changes according to the ritual calendar and displays harvest fruits and symbols of the specific season. There's the altar dedicated to gods and spirits, or the altar for ancestors and loved ones, living or dead; a place where the magic of memory is highly protective. On the altar, magical objects are arranged, such as candles, wands, knives, chalices and cauldrons, pentacles, images and photographs, incense, stones and herbs, and statuettes of gods— but there are no limits to the possibilities. On my altar, next to a wooden statue of Baba Yaga, I usually place little boxes and objects that I have had for a lifetime, those that carry memories of childhood. The last type is the portable altar, which is re-created within a box that can hold the symbols of the elements (a stone, a piece of incense, herbs or berries, a shell, etc.) and other special small items. This allows us to always have an altar nearby, in our bag or pocket.

CANDLES

. : .

Candles are one of the most common ritual objects for spells and meditation. They represent the element of fire and are generally used to purify, strengthen rituals, and visualize the object of a magical act. We can buy them or make them ourselves out of beeswax or eco-friendly waxes like soy-based wax, then add essential oils and fragrances and decorate them with flowers, herbs, pieces of stone, and crystals. In the dim flame of the candle, we remember the goodness of light, which is all the more precious when we understand how uncertain it is. A candle is a light that does not dispel darkness but simply shines, indicating a path. We are constantly surrounded by shadows, our sometimes scary, sometimes comforting companions. We let the light burn down completely for our desires. The color of the candle represents the specific area of the spell, or corresponds to the season or god invoked. Red candles represent courage and sexual love; green is prosperity; pink is romantic love; blue is health, communication, and calm; yellow is protection and cheerfulness; orange is faith in oneself; brown is a love for the earth, animals, and nature; black fights negativity and operates in darkness; and white is purity, vision, and truth. For the seasons, white, green, and pink are spring; yellow, orange, and red are summer; gold, brown, and red are autumn; and white, silver, dark blue, dark green, and black are winter.

STONES AND CRYSTALS

. : .

Stones and crystals embody the qualities of the earth since they are born and "grow" within it, sediment after sediment, touching the air and other elements. They can be purified under running water (but not all: don't use water with Anhydrite!) or by burning sage or incense. They can be recharged by placing them under the sun, stars, or a waxing or full moon. In magical practice, they are used to help heal, to encourage focus, for meditation, as talismans of protection, or to remind us that the soul should always be rooted in tangible reality. A stone grid can be placed around diviner objects, cards, and runes, not simply as decoration but to help focus answers. Personally, the stones I work with most are obsidian, selenite, malachite, amazonite, rose quartz, tiger's eye, amethyst, carnelian, and serpentine. Obsidian is my favorite because it helps confront darkness and negativity. Selenite is used to get in touch with yourself and your intuition; I use this one most often when reading tarot cards. Malachite is used to contact fate. Amazonite is for faith and to finish something you've started. Rose quartz is for your emotional and sentimental life. I have a tiger's eye necklace I wear often to remind me to maintain a connection with animals and to have courage. Amethyst is for dreams. Carnelian is a universal good luck charm that instills joy. And finally, serpentine helps re-establish balance within chaos.

TAROT CARDS

· : ·

Through the divinatory arts, we can search for contact with time—past, present, or future—or find enlightenment about ourselves and the development of a given situation. Tarot cards are some of the most popular and appealing divinatory tools. They date back to the Italian Renaissance period, whereas the occult and esoteric use of them spread throughout Europe starting in the late 18th century. There are 78 cards in a deck, divided into two groups: 22 major arcana cards, which contain archetypal figures like the Fool, the Star, and the World, and reflect the most powerful influences on life; and 56 minor arcana cards, which are connected to daily events and divided into four suits—batons (fire and imagination), cups (water and feelings), swords (air and mental strength), and pentacles (earth and practicality). These include numbered cards from ace to 10 and four court cards (King, Queen, Knight, and Jack).

With the tarot, we can go on a journey of initiation, which is often called the Fool's journey, borrowing from the card of the same name, numbered zero. The Fool is depicted as a young person who ventures toward his fate while carrying a little bag of magical objects; these objects represent potential, hope, and courage, as well as foolishness, hazards, and chaos. No card is entirely positive or negative; both are present in the figure, and it's up to the intuition and practice of a witch or wizard to interpret the message. Sometimes the deeper meanings can contradict one's first impression. Therefore, one might have to meditate on the meaning of a card by leaving it on an altar for a few days.

THE MIRROR

· ⋮ ·

It's well known that mirrors are magical and sometimes unsettling, more so than our actual appearance. Many traditions believe that they can reflect our soul, or even trap it. That's what happens to Narcissus when he looks into the water and falls in love with his own reflection, before falling in and drowning. Truth is hidden in the soul, but one must know how to embrace it. The mirror shows beauty to the stepmother of Snow White, but it's misunderstood. I believe this means something else: it invites the woman to look beyond appearances. Beauty has no age. It is found in the simplicity of a spirit that looks for joy in everything. Alice falls through the looking glass into another world. Harry Potter uses it to communicate with his dead parents. Lady Galadriel shows possible future events in her silver mirror. In China, people believe they protect against demons. In India, mirrors are used as decorations on clothes to reflect light. Shamans in Mongolia use a *toli*, a mirror made of copper, brass, or bronze, to protect themselves from evil spirits and conjure their spirit guides. Black obsidian mirrors were used by the Aztecs, and in Europe in the early modern period they were considered effective for communicating with the spiritual world. With imagination, this portal can make contact with the world where our other self lives, separate from us. We do not look into the mirror, but rather immerse ourselves in that version of us on the other side.

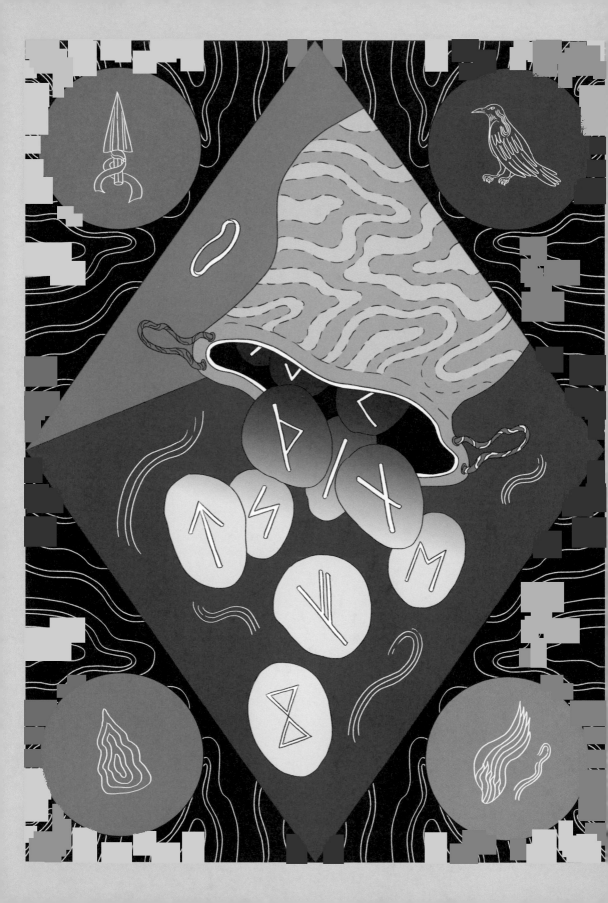

RUNES

· ∴ ·

All alphabets are magical. Each letter contains sounds and potential. Let's try something: let's forget what we know and try to look at the letters of our alphabet as if they were symbols, like the O for "orange", the V for "void", or the S for "serpentine." If you change perspective, something normal becomes extraordinary. In the community of witches and wizards, the Germanic alphabet, called *Futhark*, is commonly used. There are three versions. The oldest dates back to the 2nd century CE. It is composed of 24 letters with angular features, which makes them suitable for carving on hard materials. Stones and runic inscriptions are mainly found in Germanic areas, from Scandinavia to the British Isles and central Europe. The origin and divinatory use of runes come from Scandinavian myths. According to the poem *Hávamál*, Odin sacrificed himself to the world tree, an ash called Yggdrasil, by injuring himself with a spear and hanging by his feet for nine days in order to learn and master the secret language of knowledge, the runes, which appeared in the end. This event suggests something very important: to understand magic, one must be ready to wait, to fail, to work humbly, and sometimes to hide. My advice for working with runes is to carve or draw them on something so that you establish contact with the symbols. They are perhaps less beautiful than if you were to buy them like this, but they will thus hold the power of your hand and eyes.

ANIMALS

Something—or someone—peers out from behind a witch or wizard. It's a creature who lives in their home, anticipates their movements, and participates in their daily life. These creatures and their masters learn to speak a special language. Are they satanic, angelic, or simply themselves? In this chapter, we will explore the most common animals that safeguard the magical arts.

THE BEE

So small yet so extraordinary, the magic of bees comes first and foremost from their social structure and the role they play in maintaining the well-being of the planet. Bees live in a matriarchal society, united by a single mind that protects the heart of the hive, the queen. They are a symbol of the Great Mother, of the female power of regeneration and preservation. Thanks to this, everything is connected, and no one is useless. Every bee is also a successful alchemist: they make gold. For the Celts, this sweet gold was fermented to make the mead of the gods, a drink that united heaven and earth—considering that their tireless work could transform sunlight into thick honey. Bees are therefore associated with abundance. An old (and sad) English spell suggested carrying three dead bees in a blue bag to bring happiness, wealth, and health. Fortunately, in recent times, this practice has replaced the real bees with ceramic figurines. More importantly, these animals are messengers between worlds and between people. When they are seen in a home, it heralds good visits; if someone dies, telling the bees is a way to quickly let everyone know so that they can say their final good-byes.

THE DOG

The dog, unsurprisingly, is one of the most common animal familiars of the witch. When one came across a dog in the company of individuals who were part of a presumed community of magical—and satanic—arts, the dog's loyalty made it the perfect suspect. In fact, in some Danish witch trials, the Devil was depicted as a black dog, sometimes standing on its hind legs. Some legends speak of ghostly black bloodhounds that were sent by witches from Cornwall to chase the souls of the drowned. Black dogs or hellhounds arrive at the crossroads of English villages as nocturnal ghosts to escort the dead to the afterlife. Even today, a black dog is a symbol of depression, separation, and of drastic and emotional changes, and might therefore also represent shadows—the aspect in us that remains hidden and difficult to process. It's possible that dogs are harmed by their association with sadness and death, which comes from their loyalty to humans, the unconditional love they give even when abused. They are thus also great spirit guides. They point you in the direction of healing, even when passing through pain and fear, only to realize that behind the image of a demon is the face of a friend, an enduring protection.

THE GOAT

I remember a story from my childhood imagination in which I scaled a rocky slope in the mountains alongside a goat. Some magical friendships begin in dreams and memories, only to be reawakened before the Dark Lord, portrayed as a black goat. The black goat appears in the upside-down pentagram on the forehead of Baphomet, the demon of sexuality that the animal is associated with. Sexual perversion was one of the central themes in accusations of witchcraft; witches sealed their pacts with matters of the flesh with Satan and the devils. But sexuality also means primitive energy, reinvigorated nature, ecstasy. This symbolism made the goat very dear to the gods and supernatural creatures of the fields, plains, and forests before it became a satanic image. Let's close our eyes and imagine Pan, a faun, who walked on goat hooves, swayed his horns, and played his flute to calm animals and protect shepherds. He had one body, but it was half-goat, half-human. Perhaps the goat represents our inner child: never truly tamed, in tune with the smells and life of the outdoors, in tune with Pan—with everything.

THE HORSE

One tradition stipulates that a horseshoe, which is moon-shaped, protects against curses and the evil eye. This is the most common magical trait associated with horses. Witches would braid their manes, a habit borrowed from fairies, and ride them wildly at night. Equine transformation was one of the gifts of witches, who could take on the appearance of a black horse—but it was also used as a curse. Swedish witches were said to have put halters on sleeping men, turning them into horses that they would then ride to exhaustion. Horses are spooked by the dark. A demon called a mare would ride on a sleeping person, causing nightmares. Some enchanted horses were said to be best avoided, like the Scottish Kelpie, which would appear docile but become agitated as soon as someone tried to mount it; this would cause it to run madly and hurl the person into water, possibly drowning them. In Greek mythology, these animals pulled the chariots of Poseidon under the sea, and of Apollo as he journeyed to the sun. Whether through the sky, below the waves, or at night, horses run freely and reawaken our fear and desire.

THE BOAR

In one Arthurian story, Merlin goes mad and begins to wander the forests with a wolf and a boar. In Nordic tradition, Gullinbursti was a golden boar of the gods that shone so strongly, it could dispel the shadows of winter. On Earth, a common boar was sacrificed on the winter solstice as a symbol of the fading sun, leaving room for new light. Light arrives in the animal with wild exuberance, evoking a return of something that has long been hidden. The boar recalls honor and battle despite not being of a predatory nature, and its tusks were used to make special protective amulets. The domestic variety had much clearer witch-like traits. The Devil sometimes takes on the appearance of a black boar, and some legends claim that witches could transform into swine. For the Celts, the dead ate pork once they arrived on the other side in order to integrate into their second lives. But sows, both wild and domestic, take the magical cake: a white sow was the animal companion of Ceridwen, the witch queen and Welsh goddess of rebirth and the dead, who would blend prophecy and poetic inspiration in her cauldron.

THE RAVEN

In England, you should always greet a raven when it crosses your path on the street or in a park. It would be very rude not to! This is an indication of the animal's mythological reputation. Common sense might say that they bring bad luck, and of course, the raven is associated with death due to its feeding habits. But its connection to death in magical tradition means that the raven can see far across different worlds, change form, acquire knowledge, and preserve long-lasting memories from the past. The ravens Huginn and Muninn (Thought and Memory) sat on the shoulders of the Scandinavian god Odin, who protected wanderers, fortune-tellers, and wizards. They brought the god information about everything. Morrigan, the Irish god of battle and prophecy, could take the form of a raven. And for the Native Americans, whose traditions have often been incorporated into the practices of modern-day witches, these animals were considered tricksters—unreliable divine buzzkills that dared to disturb the balance by fostering new knowledge among humans. The raven is the color of night, dreams, the wisdom of the dead, and the magic of transformation. Having a raven as an ally allows one to walk safely through the shadows.

THE SEAL

Maybe it's the gloomy expression, but seals possess an enchanted aspect that merges with something human, reminding humans of themselves. The selkies in particular come to mind. Stories about the selkies are common along the coasts of Ireland and Scotland, particularly on the archipelagos of Orkney and the Hebrides. A selkie is a therianthropic creature, which means they can change between human and seal form by shedding their skin. It's not a curse; they are simply both at the same time. There are selkies of both sexes, but the most famous legends are about the female ones. They are meek and agreeable, with the wild nostalgia of the sea in their eyes. One popular tale says that if a man steals their skin, the selkie will become the man's wife until they rediscover their skin—perhaps among the rafters of an attic, in an old chest, or under a boat in the garage. They will then don their skin again and reunite with their people, sometimes followed by their children, who have inherited their metamorphic nature. The magic of selkies and seals is in the soul, our true clothes. This soul rises from the depths, from the secret every person contains, which is as distant as the ocean is wide, and makes us shine, giving us the form we need to live in the world.

THE CAT

The cat is often thought of as a witch's companion. Sneaky, unpredictable, nocturnal, intuitive, guardian of the home, independent, and capable of deep affection, the cat is a sly observer. The cat and witch have been synonymous since ancient times. The Egyptian goddess Bastet, protector of the domestic realm and birth, has the head of a cat. The Nordic goddess of beauty and fertility, Freya, is associated with the cat, whereas the Hindu goddess of giving birth, Shasthi, rides on one. Not all cats are familiars, though all are great adventure companions. Every cat I have ever had has left a special imprint on my life, but some have also revealed themselves to be masters of magic, teaching me a stronger connection to the common language, and, more importantly, to see in the dark, which gave me an appreciation for the nocturnal qualities of things. Negative tales claim that cats would suck the breath of children while they slept. If we reinterpret this, we can say that they share the intimacy of breathing with us—that invisible act that makes us feel alive. The magic of cats is the magic of the home as a spiritual and physical place. They are the guardians of our places and our souls.

THE OWL

The barn owl, long-eared owl, tawny owl, and little owl are all disguised witches and wizards. They live all around the world, peering into the night, waiting for the chance to strike their sleeping prey. They look like ghosts and have special feathers that make their wings silent. They are more closely connected to the dark side of magic than any other animal. They represent life in the dark and the death and fear that exists within it. Their cry has often been likened to the scream of an evil demon, or considered an omen of bad fate. In ancient Greece, they were the animals of the goddess Athena, patron of war and wisdom. What wisdom comes from owls? Difficult and long-lasting wisdom. They are lone hunters, so they help to develop independence, sharpen the senses, encourage us to linger on dreams and intuition rather than fleeing from them, and to appreciate loneliness as a place where you can discover truth and overcome anxiety. In the film *Labyrinth*, the goblin king Jareth, played by David Bowie, transforms into a barn owl to fly between worlds. Those who are friends of the owl know that we walk in multiple connected dimensions in life.

THE HARE

Some tales claim that witches would steal milk from cows, ransack the harvest, and commit other misdeeds in the homes of neighbors in the form of a hare. A hare standing alert on its hind legs or attentive to a cry in a frightening moment might look like a miniature human, some sort of supernatural being spying on the business of the nearby village before returning to their den. Isobel Gowdie of Scotland, who was tried in the Highlands in 1662, claimed she could transform into a hare in the name of the Devil to do her curses before returning home. But the magical power of hares (and rabbits) is not only in the transformation of witches. According to Chinese mythology, a hare lives on the moon, mixing an elixir for long life in a small mortar and protecting wild animals with its satellite. Rabbits and hares are sacred to the goddesses of love in both Greco-Roman mythology (Aphrodite or Venus) and Nordic mythology (Freya). The Germanic goddess of spring, Eostre, chose them as companions. Talismans in the form of hares and rabbits protect personal transformations and fertility, and represent courage in moments of need.

THE WOLF

⏝

With its gray coat and yellow eyes, the wolf is one of the most misunderstood animals in Europe. It was exterminated in Scotland in the 18th century and continues to be persecuted in many places on the continent. History has not been kind to wolves. Witches of the past were accompanied by werewolves—men accused of turning into the beasts and slaughtering farm animals. They were given a belt by the Dark Lord and would transform at crossroads or in forests after making the traditional pact with him. This is the type of wolf Little Red Riding Hood meets when she steers off the right path. However, if we look beyond this, we find an inner teacher, an animal that can always find the way. In many Native American cultures, wolves are associated with "medicine" (spiritual healing), and the magic inherent in the natural world. They are also one of the animals most closely connected to the Scandinavian god Odin, for whom they represent shamanic and mysterious aspects. A wolf knows how to behave in packs, highly respectful of the group while also defending its solitude. As in the modern English fable by Angela Carter, I like to think that when you get lost in the woods, you aren't eaten by a wolf but rather learn a new form of trust by following the wild animal.

THE COW

If you are walking in the grass and come across a cow as white as the moon with ears as red as blood, beware—it could be cursed, or perhaps a transformed Morrigan, the guardian of battle and protector of the ancient Irish people. The cow was also important to the Irish goddess Brigid, the bright opposite of the Morrigan. Likewise, the animal is sacred to female divinities that protect mothers and the family in various traditions. On the Indian subcontinent, the cow is extremely sacred. In the Mediterranean, the bull embodies both the daily power of the sun and dark, terrestrial strength, like in the legend of the Minotaur, the cannibal man-bull hybrid locked in the labyrinth, a symbol of destiny. The mother goddesses in ancient Egypt often had the faces or horns of cows, which looked like a crescent moon. Cow and bull, moon and sun, they take care of others and beat their hooves to the rhythm of the day. They were a target of witches in the past, so seeing them in a field next to a hare was a bad omen. We obtain food from cows, both milk and meat. Their submissiveness is a lesson in respecting life, one that some of us feed off.

THE TOAD

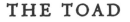

We might search for a witch and instead find a toad in the shadows. In my mountain town, I have seen many! They are often greeted with shivers of fear because we might think we can be transformed into one—or they into us, perhaps after receiving a kiss. They are often associated with the fly agaric mushroom, or the iconic toadstool. Together, they represent an omen of hallucinations and intoxication, or of visions and revelations, depending on the interpretation. In folkloric medicine, the animal has an unhappy (and ineffective) fate. It was one of the preferred animals used for cures that involved transferring illnesses from humans to animals. For example, to stop excessive bleeding from the nose, a toad was pierced and put in a small bag to wear around the neck while repeating ritual words along with the names of Christ, the Virgin Mother, and the saints, until the toad had fully dried up. At that point, the bleeding would have stopped.

Despite these violent practices, the magic of the toad depends on elements like mud and humidity, which guarantee the fertility of the earth. Finally, one ancient legend says that a diamond is hidden in the head of a toad. We see beauty with love and respect before we see it with our eyes.

THE SALMON

The salmon isn't one of the classic companions of witches and wizards; however, it's worth including it in our list of magical animals if we consider its characteristics. In Celtic beliefs, a salmon swimming calmly in spring water acquires sacred knowledge when it swallows nine nuts from the nearby sacred tree. This is the knowledge of those who dare to fight against the stream. The fish embodies the river but pushes in the opposite direction, toward its origin, moving upstream to procreate once it is in its earlier home. A witch or wizard today who turns to a salmon for guidance is prepared to fight for their ideals, knowing that we find our willpower with humility and perseverance. Fighting the current means inverting natural processes. The dead become memory, inspiration, and guidance. They are remembered, literally carried in the heart. The salmon directs us to the path of our return, closing a circle that began by accident and ended with dreams and vocation. Every journey is magical because it takes us home, to our birth, to where our life is held in the palm of a hand, like a nut.

THE SNAKE

The snake goddesses were forebears of witches. A Cretan figurine from 1600 BCE depicts a goddess with a cat head and two snakes in her hands, alternating reproduction and caducity. According to Jewish myths, the snake that tempted Eve was the transformation of Adam's first wife, Lilith. These animals are demons, poisonous. However, without the snake, the human would not have eaten from the fruit of good and evil—the symbol of free will. In the sanctuary of Delphi, the Pythia or "Pythoness" took her name from a mysterious oracular serpent, which was sometimes depicted as being defeated by Apollo, or otherwise simply placed next to the god. Two intertwined serpents were found on the caduceus of Hermes, a symbol of balance. A single snake wrapped around a branch is the symbol of Asclepius, god of medicine. In French legend, the water fairy Melusine takes on a hybrid woman-snake—or woman-amphibian—form once a week. The bond between this animal and water is found in the regenerative power of both. Water is the substance of life, and the snake is the animal of knowledge. Only those who experience the limits of mortality can acquire this knowledge.

PRACTICES
AND SPELLS

This chapter offers advice for putting your art into practice, with a focus on shared moments of ritual for the magical community. For example, it looks at how you might work with the moon or dreams; what you should carry in your amulet bag; how you can use magic to heal, create, share, or simply find refuge, so that you can restore your spirit in difficult moments.

THE WHEEL OF THE YEAR

~ ~ ~

The Wheel of the Year is the seasonal calendar of eight festivities or sabbaths. These include Yule (December 21, winter solstice), Imbolc (February 1, Candlemas), Ostara (March 21, spring equinox), Beltane (May 1), Litha (June 21, summer solstice), Lammas (August 1), Mabon (September 21, autumn equinox), Samhain (October 31, Hallowe'en). These days follow the rhythms of the sun and the energy of the earth, which prospers and dreams. The veil between worlds becomes thinner at these moments, and your magical work is thus strengthened. Yule celebrates the progressive return of light and is a moment of human warmth and sharing; Imbolc pays homage to the first reawakening of the earth; Ostara is spring, the equinox between the dark and light; Beltane is the festival of fire, welcoming the coming summer; Litha is the triumph of light and the chosen time to contact fairies; Lammas is the first harvest of the fields; Mabon is the autumnal abundance and harvest; Samhain is the ending of the year with the harvest of meat, during which candles are displayed and windows are left ajar so that ancestors who visit feel welcome. All magic and rituals are more effective during the sabbaths. But it can also be a good time to dedicate ourselves to decorating an altar and domestic spaces, and preparing food and gifts.

THE MOON

~ ~ ~

We observe the completion and rebirth of the life cycle in the moon. Long before the sun, the moon was used to regulate farming, dictating its rhythms. Likewise, magic can follow the rhythms of the moon. The new moon is great for developing projects and setting your dreams free; the waxing moon is for implementing ideas and improving your psycho-physical state; the full moon is the most powerful phase, during which desires are granted and every spell is strengthened; the waning moon allows us to look inward and try to process difficulties and remove obstacles. And the black moon is ambiguous. For some, it is particularly favorable, whereas for others, its potential is too destructive and marks a time to stop.

Each month has its special moon, to which you can dedicate meditation, a poem, or a collage called a "moonboard." These are the names of the most common moons: Wolf Moon (January); Snow Moon (February); Worm Moon (March); Pink Moon (April); Flower Moon (May); Honey Moon (June); Deer Moon (July); Sturgeon Moon (August); Harvest Moon (September); Hunter's Moon (October); Beaver Moon (November); Oak Moon (December).

DREAMS

~ ~ ~

Many follow the Dreaming Way as the path for looking inward, into the unconscious, where lines fade and we find ourselves in a strange mess of places, time, and bodies. In some dreams, we have the feeling that we are receiving a message. Others persistently return, asking us to resolve an enigma or face our fears. In them, animals might run by our side or we might transform into them. The best tool for the world of dreams is a diary, and it's best if you have one dedicated to this activity. Keep it next to your bed so that you can write down everything when you wake up. Some dreams tend to disappear with the confusion of the day. Train yourself to remember. One nice exercise is a "dreamboard," a collage you can create in your diary with figures, photos, and writings that help you retell or decode a dream. To foster revealing dreams, empty your mind before bed, seek darkness, and create a space for your vision free of feelings. During the day, try to interpret them with tarot cards. Search for images from your dream in the cards. Use only three or five cards. Then write down your impressions and thoughts.

CREATING A MAGIC BAG

~~~

The magic bag hangs from the belt of a witch or wizard. It holds their spells. You can create your own for two purposes: for propitiatory and protective spells, or as a bag of memories and personal power. In the first case, choose two square pieces of cloth of your favorite color and a bit of string. Sew the two pieces together and fill the bag with herbs, crystals, berries, shells, symbols of the elements, and meaningful objects, such as dice, little dolls, or a photo. You can add a written message with your intentions for the bag as well. Then tie it up with the string. You can recharge it under the moon, choosing whichever phase you find most suitable.

The other version of the bag is one you might have inherited, received as a gift, or bought yourself. I have a leather one that I have had since I was seven. I put old pendants, rings, and berries from my forest in it. Fill it with various objects, including gifts from important people in your life. It will become your bag of time.

THE MAGIC OF KNOTS

~ ~ ~

Historically, one of the most effective magical practices has been the use of knots, whether enchanted or bewitched knots, nautical knots, or simple string knots. Some traditions say that finding feathers from your pillow knotted up is a bad sign that someone has given you the evil eye! When horsehair or your own hair becomes knotted, it is said that elves have played with it during the night! Then there are the coastal wizards who sell winds to sailors in the form of knots, loosening and tying them as requested.

The spell I recommend is very popular and doesn't involve anything evil. It is the creation of a Witch's Ladder, a talisman imbued with your essence. In the past, a cord of braided hair was used. You can, however, use twine or string in your favorite color. Choose an odd number of small objects, such as pendants, feathers, dried flowers, shells, or stones, depending on your intention or the entity you wish to dedicate your talisman to. Tie the objects to the string with knots. They will then hold your power. Use the talisman while you do your magic, or as protection.

LOVE CHARMS

~ ~ ~

Juniper berries can flavor any type of love. One charm from the witches of Cornwall suggests stringing 49 juniper berries on a green string, alternating them with knots. Hang the garland on a door of your house to attract love, or inside your house to strengthen a love that already exists. More simply, you can carry six juniper berries with you in a bag tied with a green string.

Why juniper? The bush is associated with the element of fire, and therefore, with the courage of feelings. Its Greek name, *arkeuthos*, means "distancing danger." In the Old Testament, the prophet Elijah seeks refuge under the branches of a juniper bush as he flees from Queen Jezebel, and there he meets an angel. In one fairy tale from the Brothers Grimm, a juniper tree protects the love between a brother and sister after they die, killed by their stepmother, until the boy is reborn again.

Try this method to find love: get two small rose quartz hearts, a red fabric bag, some white string, and a pink candle. Charge the hearts under the light of the candle and have it burn out completely. Put the hearts in the bag and tie it with the string, then carry it with you wherever you go.

TAROT AND ORACLE READING

~ ~ ~

Here are some suggestions you can use for your deck of tarot cards. First, find a physical or mental space where you can concentrate, then shuffle the cards and ask a question. Remember that tarot cards don't answer questions with a clear yes or no: they offer a path you can follow. Take out one card for some quick advice, or lay down three cards, which represent the past, present, and future—or the situation, the obstacle, and the development. Search for a message with your intuition. Take a photo or write down the cards to think about them in the following days. Trust your instincts, even when they seem to distance themselves from guidebooks. Establish a personal relationship with the deck and dare to redefine the images.

You can do the same with oracles, whether they are cards or objects. If you are working with runes, you can draw them blindly from a bag, one or three as with the cards, and follow the same procedure. You can also draw an unspecified number and throw them on the table, then choose to interpret the ones that fall face up. Consult a guidebook, but also listen to your interpretation.

THE MAGIC OF CANDLES

~ ~ ~

The single light of a candle is powerful magic. It creates hope. Here are two simple spells you can do with these objects. The first is generic and works with any objective. Choose a colored candle depending on what your desire is (see the instruments chapter on candles for a brief description of the meanings of different colors). Hold the candle in your hands to fill it with your intentions, then light it and put it in a candle holder. It's preferable to use a match for lighting your candle. Place your palms near the flame (without burning your hands) and absorb a bit of its heat. Lastly, let the candle burn up completely.

The other spell is useful for freeing yourself of any fears you might have. Write your feelings or a situation you wish to resolve on a piece of paper. Light a black candle if you want to eliminate the obstacle completely, or a white candle if you want to see the problem more clearly. Focus on the flame for a few minutes. Burn the piece of paper in a fire-resistant container. Then let the candle burn out completely. Spread the ashes somewhere outside.

CHARMS FOR ANIMALS

~ ~ ~

Witches and wizards have a very strong connection with animals. Here are two charms you can use to protect your domestic friends as well as more elusive and wild companions. The first is focused on curing animals close to us. Get a container with a lid and fill it with the animal's food, such as kibble or seeds. At some quiet moment during the day, go to where the animal spends its time, like the garden, a cage, or a specific room. Play the container like a musical instrument and repeat the name of the animal along with the words "Be protected, calm, and healthy" in a whisper four times.

The other spell is used to prevent domestic animals from getting lost or being taken away. Take three hairs or feathers from the animal and tie them together with a red string and make nine knots. Then repeat the animal's name, followed by the words "Always return to me." Put everything in a red bag and hang it somewhere outside where the animal spends time.

THE MAGIC OF HERBS

~~~

Drinking a cup of herbal tea is a daily ritual that can prove deeply magical. Every herb has some quality that affects the mind and the body. You can collect your herbs or buy them at a herbalist's shop. I suggest trying to grow some in your garden or a planter, or foraging for common ones. You will learn something from this that will make your magic stronger. Dry the herbs out and mix them together. You can also add tea leaves. Here are some examples of their effects: mint regenerates the spirit and provides enthusiasm; dandelion roots are perfect for the magic of dreams; orange peel helps attract material fortune. Ginger is for trusting yourself and taking on new experiences. Nettle purifies the blood and spirit, distancing danger and unpleasant feelings, just as the plant's stingers do to those who clumsily handle it. Mugwort, the queen of spells, attracts visions, facilitating divination and psychic abilities. And finally, hawthorn flowers, from an enchanted tree, help with love.

THE MAGIC OF STARS

~ ~ ~

To work your magic with the stars, that's often all you need. Make a wish during a shooting star. Lie down in the grass and look at the sky until your pain and worries become as light as air and fly away. Lose yourself in their ancestral light. In some myths, the stars are just holes in the sky that filter light from other worlds. After death, our spirit walks along the stars or crosses through the holes to reunite with ancestors. This timeless light is what we are searching for in our spells.

Here are two suggestions for carrying the stars with you. For the first, you need a small silver bell. Display it under the stars to purify it, then tie it to your ankle, wrist, or around your neck, or place it in a white bag. The sound represents the words of the stars, which are always with you. For the second spell, you need a bucket of water. Put it outside on a starry night. In the morning, wash your face with the water of the stars to brighten your soul and foster trust in yourself.

THE MAGIC OF GOOD LUCK

~ ~ ~

For good luck, carry a four-leaf clover or lucky stone with you. You can also carry a penny because luck exists in humble forms.

If you want something more elaborate, here are two charms. For the first, you can tie small bells to a string and display it during a waxing moon. When the moon is full, place the garland wherever you spend the most time in your house. When it jingles, the bells will bring good luck. For the second charm, get a green candle and black candle. The black represents bad luck; the green, good luck. Tie a knot on some twine and light the black candle. Put the knot in the flame until it burns up. Say "I cast away my bad luck!" and then blow out the candle. Now, light the green one and sprinkle a bit of salt over it. You can place an object like a bracelet or pendant under the light before wearing it. Then say "My luck will shine!" and let it burn out.

THE MAGIC
OF HEALING

~ ~ ~

Every spell can heal as it moves through the inner worlds or those beyond. However, regarding moments of deep sadness, in addition to possible medical or psychological help, sometimes we can do something to help ourselves. Writing in a diary is a way to vent our feelings, one word at a time. Or you can play an instrument, like a drum, which is used by many witches today. Try to find your rhythm with it. Lastly, you can use a gemstone that represents you, along with a blue or white candle and some salt. Place the stone in a cup of salt for a few minutes. The salt evokes the earth, from which all things derive. Light the candle. Take the stone and pass it over the flame to absorb its energy. The flame represents pain, which harms and purifies at the same time. Replace the crystal in the salt and put it under the light of the candle until it has burned out completely. Then put the stone back in the salt so it can restore the pain to the earth. Leave it there as long as you like. Then, carry the stone with you, or put it in a secret place. However, don't forget the sadness—it is part of you, but it cannot take away your spirit.

COMMUNICATING WITH THE SPIRITS AND FAIRIES

~ ~ ~

Perhaps you want to contact specific spirits in your magic. Here are some ways you can approach them. For ancestors and spirits of the dead, you can use a photo placed in the center of a circle of seven white candles. Put a cup of water next to the image for those who have passed recently. The spirit is thirsty at the beginning of its journey. Whisper kind words.

If you wish to approach those who live on the threshold, like fairies and elves, pay attention to what they will tell you, because they are unpredictable. Don't ever go to them directly! Use names like Good People, Moss People, or Sea Dwellers. Be kind. The best moments to contact them are at dawn, twilight, or when Venus rises or sets. Remember that you can meet the Good People anywhere: in the attic, the forest, or behind an old store. Leave them offerings of milk, honey, or vegetable soup, at certain times and in the same place. Perhaps they won't ever see them—but they know everything about you.

PRAYING TO THE TREES

~ ~ ~

Trees are the guardians of life. They have centuries-old wisdom and ancient faces. They protect the breath of the earth. They seem human when they open their arms to the sky. Never tire of thanking the trees through prayer and blessings.

Here are some ways you can work with them. First, think about them. Go where they grow and choose one to focus on. Allow it to be your teacher. Watch it, learn its shape, sense its inner movements. The tree will bring you peace and unblock long-hidden emotions. Then, try to contact it. Hug the plant and feel its lifeblood under the bark, like water in your body. Sense that you, we, are not alone in this world. Lastly, one magical tradition that comes from the British Isles says to tie colorful strips of fabric to the branches of certain plants. These represent prayers and desires, often regarding fertility, creativity, and matters of physical and mental health. Tie a human object to the tree so that the two forces can communicate. Wherever you might go, the tree remains stable, and so does your prayer.

~ ~ ~

BIBLIOGRAPHY

This bibliography is minimal and conceived as a compass to orient oneself in the universe of magical publications among historical data, texts of rituals, contemporary traditions, and, of course, myths and eternal tales.

About the history of witchcraft and magic:

Apps, Lara, and Andrew Gow, *Male Witches in Early Modern Europe*, Manchester University Press, Manchester and New York 2003.

Davies, Owen, *Popular Magic: Cunning-folk in English History*, Hambledon Continuum, London 2003.

Ginzburg, Carlo, *The Night Battles: Witchcraft & Agrarian Cults in the Sixteenth & Seventeenth Centuries*, Routledge, London 2015.

Howe, Ellic, *The Magicians of the Golden Dawn*, Samuel Weiser, York Beach 1984.

Hutton, Ronald, *The Triumph of the Moon: A History of Modern Pagan Witchcraft*, Oxford University Press, Oxford 1999.

———, *The Witch: A History of Fear, from Ancient Times to the Present*, Yale University Press, New Haven 2017.

Introvigne, Massimo, *Il cappello del mago*, Sugarco, Milan 1990.

Matteoni, Francesca, *Il famiglio della strega. Sangue e stregoneria nell'Inghilterra moderna*, Aras, Fano 2014.

Messana, Maria Sofia, *Inquisitori, negromanti e streghe nella Sicilia moderna (1500-1782)*, Sellerio, Palermo 2007.

Pereira, Michela, *Arcana sapienza. Storia dell'alchimia occidentale dalle origini a Jung*, Carocci, Rome 2019.

About contemporary magic and its practices:

Buckland, Raymond, *The Witch Book: The Encyclopedia of Witchcraft, Wicca, and Neopaganism*, Visible Ink Press, New York 2002.

Cabot, Laurie, *The Witch in Every Woman: Reawakening the Magical Nature of the Feminine to Heal, Protect, Create, and Empower*, Delta, London 1997.

Cunningham, Scott, *Earth, Air, Fire, and Water: More Techniques of Natural Magic*, Llewellyn Publications, St. Paul, Minn. 1996.

Gary, Gemma, *Traditional Witchcraft: A Cornish Book of Ways*, Troy Books, London 2008.

Mooney, Thorn, *Traditional Wicca: A Seeker's Guide*, Llewellyn Publications, St. Paul, Minn. 2018.

Starhawk, *The Spiral Dance: A Rebirth of the Ancient Religion of the Great Goddess*, Harper Collins, San Francisco 1999.

Valiente, Doreen, *Natural Magic*, Robert Hale, London 1999.

About stories, myths, and folklore:

Afanasyev, Alexander N., *Russian Fairy Tales*, The Planet, London 2013.

Anderson, Sophie, *The House with Chicken Legs*, Usborne Publishing, London 2018.

Bates, Brian, *The Way of Wyrd*, Hay House, London 2013.

Blake, William, *The Complete Poems*, Penguin, London 1977.

Carter, Angela, *Nell'antro dell'alchimista*, Fazi, Roma 2019.

De Boron, Robert, *Merlin and the Grail: Joseph of Arimathea, Merlin, Perceval*, Boydell & Brewer, Martlesham 2005.

Gaiman, Neil, *Norse Mythology*, W. W. Norton & Company, New York 2017.

Malory, Thomas, *King Arthur and his Knights: Selected tales*, Oxford University Press, London and New York 1975.

Shakespeare, William, *The Tempest*, W. W. Norton & Company, New York 2019.

White, Terence Hanbury, *The Sword in the Stone*, Philomel Books, New York 1993.

Yeats, William Butler, *The Celtic Twilight*, Cosimo Classics, New York 2004.

Zimmer Bradley, Marion, *The Mists of Avalon*, Ballantine Books, New York 2003.

FRANCESCA MATTEONI

✳ ✳ ✳

Francesca is an Italian poet, writer, and historian. She has worked as a researcher in England, studying the witch trials, the magic of bodies, and medical folklore in modern times. She leads workshops on tarot readings and poetry and teaches History of Religion and Magic at some American universities in Florence. Some of her most recent publications include the book *Dal Matto al Mondo. Viaggio Poetico Nei Tarocchi* (effequ, 2019); the poetry collection *Libro di Hor* (Vydia, 2019) with images by Ginevra Ballati; an essay in *La Scommessa Psichedelica* (Quodlibet, 2020) edited by Federico di Vita; and the poetry collection *Ciò Che il Mondo Separa* (Marcos y Marcos, 2021).

ELISA MACELLARI

✳ ✳ ✳

An Italian-Thai illustrator, Elisa has worked for Italian and international publishers and magazines since 2012. Her latest books include a graphic novel called *Papaya Salad* (BAO Publishing, 2018) and the graphic biography *Kusama, Ossessioni, Amori e Arte* (Centauria Libri, 2020). She won the Autori di Immagini Gold Medal in the publishing category in 2017 and the Silver Medal in the comic category in 2019. Her work has been exhibited in Italy and abroad.